Study Guide

MACROECONOMICS

Study Guide
John S. Irons
Amherst College

MACROECONOMICS
David C. Colander
Edward N. Gamber

Upper Saddle River, New Jersey 07458

Executive editor: Rod Banister
Assistant editor: Marie McHale
Production editor: Wanda Rockwell
Manufacturer: Courier (Bookmart Press, Inc.)

ISBN 0-13-033438-3

10 9 8 7 6 5 4 3 2 1

TABLE OF CONTENTS

NOTE TO STUDENTS

This study guide was prepared to help you work your way through the textbook's ideas and models. Each chapter includes several sections to reinforce and extend the material in the text.

The best way to really learn the material is to "play" with each idea, each model, and each policy. Ask lots of what-if questions such as "what if such-and-such curve were flat," "what if policy X and policy Y were followed at the same time," etc.... This study guide will give you a start in that direction.

Summaries
Each chapter presents a summary of the material presented in the textbook. It is best to use these summaries as a review, and certainly not as a substitute for reading the textbook.

Hints/Tips/Tricks
Throughout the study guide are a variety of tips and hints. Many of the hints suggest alternative ways to think about a topic. These suggestions should complement the material in the textbook. Many of the tricks will give you a mathematical tool that will come in handy when you start to attack some of the problems. Many of these tricks will seem far a field at first, but they will make your life easier down the road.

Multiple Choice Questions
These are designed to provide you with a review of the reading. These questions focus on main concepts and definitions. In addition to knowing the correct answer, I would also suggest that you know why the other options are incorrect. The answer section will provide a brief comment on each question.

True/False/Uncertain
This section of problems gives you a set of statements that may sound reasonable. You should decide if they are true or false, or if there is some ambiguity involved. The trick to these questions is not simply getting the T/F/U answer correct, but rather understanding *why* it is true or false. If it is false, you should try to figure out why it is false, and then determine what change might make it true.

For example:

> Q: "The sky is green"
> A: False, because the sky is *blue*.

> Q: "*10*X* equals 20"
> A: Uncertain; if $X = 2$ this would be true; otherwise it is false.

Internet
The Internet exercises are designed to ask you questions that can be answered by getting on the Internet and doing some legwork.

Data/graph. Many of the questions ask you to manipulate data of one kind or another. Getting your hands on a spreadsheet program will allow you to analyze the data and easily construct graphs. There are two basic kinds of graphs you will be asked to produce. The first is a time-series graph in which values are plotted against time. The second kind is a cross-plot graph in which one data series is plotted against values in another data series. On this graph, each data point represents one period in time (for example the empirical Phillips curve is a cross-plot). Time-series graphs are useful to get a sense of what happened historically to a particular piece of data. Cross plots are useful when looking at relationships between variables.

Suggestions for web sites are given, but feel free to find others.

Problems
The problems will provide numerical examples of models presented in the chapter, or will ask you to use the models to answer various kinds of questions. They will occasionally ask you to analyze strange special cases, or will point out an interesting result. After finishing a question, I would recommend taking a step back to try to see the big picture behind the numerical results.

Good Luck!

John S. Irons
Amherst College
Amherst, MA 01002

INTERNET SITES

Many of the questions below will ask you to find some data or some other information on the web. Here are a few places to begin your search.

General Guides

Economics at About.com
http://econommic.about.com

Resources for Economists on the Internet
http://www.rfe.org

WebEc
http://www.helsinki.fi/WebEc/

Data

Bureau of Labor Statistics
http://stats.bls.gov/datahome.htm

Bureau of Economic Analysis
http://www.bea.doc.gov/

The Dismal Scientist
http://www.dismal.com

Economics and Statistics Administration
http://www.esa.doc.gov/

Federal Reserve Board
http://www.federalreserve.gov

FedStats
http://www.fedstats.gov/

Foreign Data

OECD Economics
http://www.oecd.org/eco/eco/

IMF
http://www.imf.org
(World Economic Outlook Database)

White House Economic Data
http://www.whitehouse.gov/fsbr/esbr.html

World Bank
http://worldbank.org/data/

News

CNN fn - Economy
http://cnnfn.cnn.com/news/economy/

The Economist Magazine
http://www.economist.com/

Others

Economic Report of the President
http://w3.access.gpo.gov/eop/index.html

Ray Fair's Macroeconomic Model
http://fairmodel.econ.yale.edu/

Growth Resources
http://www.nuff.ox.ac.uk/economics/growth/

CHAPTER 1.
INTRODUCTION

OBJECTIVES

1. Define macroeconomics.
2. List four goals of macroeconomics.
3. Summarize the United States' recent experience with output, inflation, unemployment, interest rates, the budget balance, and the trade balance.
4. Discuss the relationship between models and vision.
5. Describe policies designed to affect the demand side and the supply side of the economy.
6. Explain why potential output and the natural rate of unemployment are important concepts for macro policy.

CHAPTER OVERVIEW

The introduction is designed to give you a feel for some of the important policy goals that will be expanded upon in the rest of the book. It also describes the general ideas behind the tools that will be used to address these policy issues.

A good place to start is with a definition of the field: Macroeconomics is the study of issues that affect the economy as a whole, especially unemployment, inflation, and economic growth.

THE POLICY SCIENCE OF MACROECONOMICS

At the heart of why we want to study macroeconomics lie a number of fundamental questions about how the economy operates and what policymakers can do to improve the lives of citizens. As a policy science, macroeconomics addresses both positive economics – the study of how the economy works – as well as normative economics – the study of what the goals of the economy should be.

THE STANDARD GOALS OF MACROECONOMICS

The ultimate goal of macroeconomics is to learn enough about the economy so that we can formulate effective policy (either monetary or fiscal) to better meet our macroeconomic goals. These goals include:

*   High growth
*   Avoiding large swings in the economy's output level
*   Low unemployment
*   Low inflation

While the goals of the macroeconomist can be (and should be) debated, the majority of the book will focus on the study of the results of policy decision, rather than on alternative formulations of these general goals. One thing to keep in mind is that politics and political institutions determine policy, and the goals of political actors may not mirror the goals highlighted above.

Finally, it should be noted that these goals might not be achievable either individually or all at the same time. Economics is fundamentally about tradeoffs, and macroeconomics is no different in this regard.

IMPORTANT CONCEPTS AND MEASURES IN MACROECONOMICS

This first chapter introduces you to the basic ideas and concepts in macroeconomics. In addition to the set of theories and analytical tools that will be presented, we also want to learn about the economy itself. As part of this, it is important to know the past experience of the U.S. economy and others around the world.

In the U.S., as in most developed countries there has been a long-run trend towards greater output over the past 50 years as measured by real Gross Domestic Product. There have also been periods of time in which GDP will grow either faster or slower than the overall trend. These fluctuations are often associated with fluctuations in unemployment, inflation, interest rates, the trade balance and other macroeconomic measures.

Macroeconomics is an attempt to understand both the underlying trends as well as fluctuations about the trend. The way we do this is by trying to understand the relationships between the various components of the macroeconomy, such as the connection between interest rates and GDP, or between unemployment and inflation.

ACHIEVING GOALS: SUPPLY-SIDE AND DEMAND-SIDE POLICIES

Once we have identified goals, we need to then find ways of pursuing those goals. Fortunately governmental institutions have been developed to give policymakers some limited control over the behavior of the macroeconomy.

- Demand-side policies affect aggregate expenditure, usually through monetary, fiscal, or trade policy; and are the focus of short-run analysis.

- Supply-side policies are directed at changing the amount an economy is capable of producing, usually through adjusting incentives to work, innovate, or advance technology; and are the focus of long-run analysis.

Policymaker's decisions about what kind of policy to follow - either expansionary or contractionary policy - are largely dependent on their estimate of the potential level of output. This estimate is usually given by the "natural rate" of unemployment – the unemployment rate that exists when the economy is at potential output and below which inflation increases. Unfortunately, neither potential output nor the natural rate is easily measured - you can't just look it up in the newspaper the way you can stock prices - and the estimates include some uncertainty and error.

THE ROLE OF MODELS IN ECONOMICS

The economy is an incredibly complex system, and it would be impossible to understand the system and all the complex interactions in its entirety. Instead, we gain an understanding of the economy through the use of models. A model is a simplified "toy economy," which is more easily understood and which captures important relationships within the real economy. Specifically, a model is a set of relationships that explain the behavior of variables. A complete model will include assumptions, endogenous variables (those that are determined within the model), and exogenous variables (those that are determined by chance, by nature, or by some other force outside the model), as well as the behavioral and causal relationships between the variables.

Since all models are simplifications, they are not perfect and there is often debate about which model is appropriate for analyzing a certain problem. A model builder's vision guides the specification and interpretation of the model.

The competitive market-clearing vision: A view of the economy that sees a perfectly competitive market as solving the complex coordination problems of the economy in a highly effective manner. Central to this vision is that prices adjust instantaneously to achieve equilibrium.

The institutional process vision: A view that sees the problems of an economy as too complicated to be solved instantaneously by perfectly competitive markets.

CONCLUSION

This first chapter provided an introduction to the way we will approach problems in macroeconomics. You should now have a feel for the goals that macroeconomic policymakers pursue and the role that models can play in macroeconomic analysis.

The next chapter will begin by looking at some of the data that macroeconomists care about.

Tip: How to study and evaluate models.

The textbook will present you with a variety of models. There are several questions to keep in mind every time you see a new model. The answers to these questions will help you to understand the theory and will let you apply the models to reality.

- What does the model try to explain? (Or, what are the endogenous variables?)

- What is the model taking as a given? (Or, what are the exogenous variables?)

- What relationships link the endogenous variables to the exogenous variable?

- What simplifications does the model make? Is the model too simple for the question at hand? Too complex? Since all models are simplifications, it is useful to keep in mind what has been ignored in order to reach a model that is simple enough to analyze effectively.

- What is the underlying vision of the model? This is often the most important, and most overlooked question that should be asked of macroeconomic models. For example, we can ask if the model is based on a vision of perfectly clearing markets, or if the model is based on a vision that investors are perfectly rational. Visions guide the construction of models, and therefore their interpretations as well.

Think of a model the way you might think of a street map. The map is a simplification of reality that will tell you where you will end up if given a starting point and some directions. Think of the starting point as the exogenous variables, and the destination as the endogenous variable.

If you are given the starting point and directions you can then use the map to find the endpoint. You would never think of memorizing a list of starting points and directions along with the destination---you would simply pull out the map when needed. The same it true with models: rather than trying to remember all the details of what happens to the economy when something like the money supply changes, it is easier to "get out" the model and trace through the effects of the change. Even the most experienced economists will pull out a pen and paper, and sketch out a diagram or two when trying to find the effect of a policy on the economy. The trick, of course, is to know which model to use.

PROBLEMS AND EXERCISES

Multiple Choice Questions

1. The goals of macroeconomic policymakers do not include:

   a. High growth
   b. Avoiding large swings in the economy's output level
   c. Low unemployment
   d. Low inflation
   e. High value for the domestic currency relative to other countries

2. Which of the following represents a supply-side policy:

   a. Monetary policy
   b. Fiscal policy
   c. Trade policy
   d. Industry deregulation

3. Over the past 50 years, the U.S. economy has grown at approximately what rate?

   a. 2.0%
   b. 3.5%
   c. 4.5%
   d. 6.0%

4. Which statement best characterizes growth in the U.S. over the last 50 years?

   a. GDP growth has been virtually constant.
   b. The U.S. has been in recession for the same number of months as it has been in expansion.
   c. The U.S. has been in recessions for fewer months than it has been in expansion.
   d. The U.S. has been in recessions for more months than it has been in expansion.

5. Economic models always include

   a. Simplifications
   b. Endogenous variables
   c. Assumptions
   d. Equations
   e. A vision

True/False/Uncertain

For each of the questions below, answer true, false, or uncertain. Explain your answer in each case.

1. The natural rate of unemployment is the rate of unemployment that policymakers try to achieve in the short-run.

2. When there is inflation, all of the prices in the economy are rising.

3. The budget balance is determined only by tax rates and government spending decisions.

4. An economic model is a simplified representation of the relationships within an economy.

5. When output is below potential, inflation tends to rise.

Internet Exercises

1. Find an example of an economic model on the Internet that is used for policy analysis and/or forecasting. What are the endogenous and exogenous variables? What assumptions is the model making? How would you describe the modeler's vision?

   One very extensive model can be found at http://fairmodel.econ.yale.edu/.

2. Data/Graphing. Find the growth rate for the economy for the past 5 years. Using only this data, what would you estimate to be the rate of growth of potential output? How does this compare to estimates of potential output over the past 50 years?

   See: http://www.bea.doc.gov/bea/dn1.htm for data.

3. Data. The U.S. has recently done well to have a relatively high rate of economic growth and low inflation. Many other countries have not fared as well.

   Find one or more countries that are currently facing:

   a. High inflation (>20% per year)
   b. Negative output growth
   c. Both high inflation and negative output growth

   See: http://www.oecd.org; http://www.imf.org; or http://www.worldbank.org

4. Visit http://www.nber.org/cycles.html. When was the last time there was a recession in the economy? How long did it last?

5. The Internet contains a wide variety of information on the current thinking of economic policymakers. Look for recent policy speeches and comments by officials at the Federal Reserve and in the President's administration to find some of the issues people are talking about.

   a. What are some of the macroeconomic challenges that currently face policymakers?

   b. Are they worried more about unemployment or about inflation?

   c. Are people worried about a government budget deficit?

   d. How do policymakers think the economy will perform in the near future?

Start with:

Federal Reserve Board: http://www.federalreserve.gov/,
Whitehouse: http://www.whitehouse.gov/, and especially the Economic Report of the President:
http://w3.access.gpo.gov/eop/index.html
The U.S. Federal budget: http://www.whitehouse.gov/omb/budget/index.html
U.S. Treasury: http://www.ustreas.gov/

CHAPTER 2.
MEASURING THE ECONOMY

OBJECTIVES

1. Define both real and nominal GDP and state the components of GDP.
2. Distinguish between the various measures of inflation.
3. Explain how the unemployment rate is calculated and describe its shortcomings.
4. Recount the U.S. and world experience with growth, business cycles, unemployment, and inflation.
5. Describe how the U.S. trade balance and the exchange rate have changed over time.

OVERVIEW

While it sometimes makes sense to talk about the economy as performing "well" or "poorly", we also often need to be much more precise in explaining exactly what we mean. As economists we are fortunate to be able to have a variety of data with which to measure the performance of the economy and to test our theories. This chapter introduces you to some of the most important of these measures including gross domestic product (GDP), inflation, and unemployment.

CENTRAL MEASURES OF THE ECONOMY

The data of macroeconomics can largely be divided into two groups: prices and quantities. At a fundamental level, these two categories correspond roughly to the division you may have seen in your microeconomics course; however, since we are now dealing with a complex collection of a large number goods and services, rather than a single market, our definitions of "prices" and "quantities" must be more complicated as well.

Total Output

Gross Domestic Product (GDP) is the most common measure of the total *quantity* of goods and services produced by the economy. Formally, GDP is a measure of the market value of all final goods and services produced within a country within a year. Since households derive their income from firms, total output is always equal to total income in the economy. The terms total output and total income are often used interchangeably since they are always equal in magnitude.

GDP can be calculated in two theoretically equivalent ways: by adding up the output of final goods and services, or adding up the income earned in the production of goods and services. The value of output can be measured by either adding up the value added by each firm, or by adding up total expenditures on goods and services.

For example, if there were many goods in the economy (G_1, G_2, ...), each with its own price (P) and quantity (Q), GDP would be calculated as

$$GDP = P_1 \times Q_1 + P_2 \times Q_2 + ... \, .$$

To avoid double counting, intermediate goods are not included in the measure of output. For example, a tire sold to as part of an automobile would be counted twice if we included both the final sale of the car, as well as the sale of the tire from the tire company to the car company. To prevent this, we can either exclude the intermediate sale, or we can add only the value added by each company.

GDP is a flow measure, that is, it measures the amount of production in a given period of time (usually a year). Finally, when measuring GDP for a given country, we only count those goods and services produced within the borders of the country.

Aside from GDP, there are other data that measure total output, including gross national product (GNP), and net national product. Measures of total output differ by the location of production; by who owns the factors of production (either domestic or foreign), and by whether or not they include depreciation or taxes. It can sometimes be confusing knowing which measure of output to use – there is no single "best" measure. The most widely used measure is GDP, but it may sometimes be better to use other measures.

Nominal vs. Real GDP. The measure above uses current prices to measure GDP; however, when we compare output in two different years, we may want to separate the effect of a quantity change from the effect of a price change. Real GDP is one way to measure output only, keeping prices at some constant level.

- Nominal GDP is a measure of total output that uses current market prices to add up total production.

- Real GDP is a measure of total output using prices that have been fixed in a base year.

Real GDP is calculated in the same way as before, except that the prices are taken from the "base" year. For example, if 1990 were the base year, then real GDP in 2001 would be calculated as

$$GDP = P_{1990} (G_1) * Q_{2001}(G_1) + P_{1990} (G_2) * Q_{2001}(G_2) + \dots .$$

Note that in the base year, real GDP equals nominal GDP. Nominal GDP can vary year to year if either prices change, and/or if quantity changes. In contrast, real GDP will change only if quantity changes.

The Price Level

From the above definitions of GDP, we can define a measure of the price level.

GDP Deflator = Nominal GDP / Real GDP.

Hint: How to Remember the Deflator.

Think of nominal GDP as $P \times Q$ and Real GDP as just Q. So dividing nominal GDP by real gives us a measure of P - the GDP deflator.

*GDP Deflator = Nominal GDP / Real GDP = (P * Q) / Q = P.*

A second common measure of prices comes from a direct survey of various prices in the economy. The Consumer Price Index (CPI) is a measure of the prices of goods and services consumers pay, and is stated as an index of base year prices.

The calculation of the CPI is done by considering a basket of goods that a "typical" consumer would purchase in a year, and then measuring the cost of purchasing that basket. By comparing the cost of the fixed basket of goods across years, we can get a measure of how prices change.

Again taking 1990 as the base year, the CPI for 2001 can be calculated as:

$$\frac{\text{Cost of the 1990 basket of goods using 2001 prices}}{\text{Cost of the 1990 basket of goods using 1990 prices}} \times 100.$$

Note that the basket used in the CPI calculation may be very different from the basket that you or people you know might typically buy.

CPI differs from the deflator in that it measures the prices of a different set of goods. The CPI is meant to capture the goods and services that are used by consumers, including imports. The deflator captures all the goods and services produced domestically, including investment, the goods purchased by the government, and exports. In addition, the CPI's basket of goods is fixed for a longer period of time.

The CPI is not a perfect measure of the change in prices. Three factors can cause the CPI to be biased in a way that causes measured inflation to be higher that a more ideal measure of prices. These are: 1) unmeasured quality improvements, 2) the introduction of new products, and 3) the ability of people to switch to purchasing cheaper goods.

Unemployment

The population can be divided up into three groups: the employed, the unemployed, and people who are out-of the labor force. Together the employed and the unemployed make up the labor force.

The unemployment rate is given by:

Unemployment rate = Unemployed / Labor force x 100.

The labor force participation rate is given by:

Labor force participation rate = Labor Force / non-institutional population x 100.

The unemployed are only those that are currently looking for work; hence, the unemployment rate does not include discouraged workers, nor does it include people who may be under-employed.

THE DATA OF MACROECONOMIC GOALS

High growth

By growth, we usually mean the average percentage change in real GDP in an economy over a long period of time. (See below for an explanation of how to calculate rates of growth). Often, GDP *per person* is the measure people use to evaluate long-run economic performance rather than just looking at GDP. Labor productivity, or output per worker, is another important measure of economic well-being in the long-run.

Avoiding Large Swings in Output

In addition to the long-run trend in output, there are also short-run fluctuations called business cycles. Output levels below trend are called recessions, while levels above the trend are called expansions. Recessions begin at a business cycle peak, and end at the trough. A common definition of a recession is a period of two or more consecutive quarters of declining real GDP.

Historically, expansions have lasted longer than recessions: in the U.S. the duration of expansions has averaged 59 months versus 11 months for recessions. There have been 9 recessions since 1947.

Low Unemployment

In the U.S., the unemployment rate since World War II has fluctuated between 3 and 10 percent. When real GDP is growing rapidly during expansions the unemployment rate tends to fall, while when real GDP is growing very slowly, or declining, the unemployment rate tends to rise.

Other developing and developed countries have experienced significant levels of unemployment as well. These rates tend to fluctuate with the business cycles. Europe has tended to see higher rates of unemployment, while Japan has experienced lower rates.

Low Inflation

When the price level, as measured by the CPI or the price deflator, is rising, the economy is said to be experiencing inflation. When the price level is falling, we experience deflation. If the inflation rate declines (say from 5% to 2%) we say that the economy is experiencing disinflation.

Modern economies usually experience some amount of inflation. Prior to 1950 there were often times when there was deflation, but those cases are more rare today. The inflation rate in the U.S. has ranged between 1.5% and 14% over the last 50 years.

Developing countries have tended to have higher rates of inflation than the developed world. Many countries have experienced periods of hyperinflation – a situation where inflation rates are very high; sometimes reaching annual percent increases in the thousands.

International Considerations

In addition to the goals listed above, policymakers may be concerned with the trade situation with other countries. The exchange rate and the trade balance are the two biggest concerns.

Over the last 50 years, the U.S. has been trading more and more with other countries: both exports and imports have been increasing. The trade balance is measured by taking exports and subtracting imports. If the balance is negative, then we are running a trade deficit. Prior to 1973 the U.S. had a trade surplus, that is, a positive trade balance: exports were greater than imports. Since then the U.S. has been running on a trade deficit.

The exchange rate measures the amount of foreign currency that can be exchanged for one unit of the domestic currency, and is used to determine the value of one currency relative to others. The units of the exchange rate are then, for example, yen per dollar or euros per dollar. Over time, different countries have used different exchange rate regimes with fixed and floating exchange rates being the two extremes. The U.S. currently has a partially flexible exchange rate, that is, a flexible rate determined by the market, but with occasional government intervention through purchase or sales of currency.

CONCLUSION

While understanding the basics of the macroeconomic data may not be the most exciting part of macroeconomics, it is vital to establishing a base on which to work, as well as a language that we can use to discuss the important relationships in the economy.

Tip. Calculating growth rates. Indexes.

Macroeconomic data is often reported in several forms. This tips and tricks section will look at how data can be stated in levels, differences, and in growth rates

Levels
Most data starts out in "level" form. GDP, for example, is stated as $9 trillion, investment might be $3 trillion, per-capita income is $25,000, and so on.

We will also often be concerned with data for a given year and indicate this with an indicator for the period in time. For example GDP in 2001 will be Y_{2001}. Generally we can write any data series for a given year t as: X_t. The entire set of data in periods 1...T will be given by the *time-series*:

$$X_1, X_2, X_3, ..., X_{t-1}, X_t, X_{t+1}, ..., X_T.$$

Differences
In addition to caring about the level, we might also care about how much the data changes over time. We might want to know how much GDP has changed from last year to this year, and we would then calculate $Y_{2001} - Y_{2000}$.

In general, a data series $X_1, ..., X_T$ can be transformed to "differences" or "changes" by forming a new series $(X_2 - X_1), (X_3 - X_2), ..., (X_t - X_{t-1}), ..., (X_T - X_{T-1})$. Note that the new series has 1 fewer data points than the original series. In general we can write

$$\Delta X = X_t - X_{t-1}.$$

Growth rates
While the differenced data gives us an idea of the absolute change, we might also be interested in the change relative to it's initial level - in other words the percentage change ($\%\Delta$) or growth rate.

In general, the annual growth rate of some data between two years, t and t+1, is

$$\%\Delta Xt = \Delta X_t / X_{t-1} = (X_t - X_{t-1}) / X_{t-1}.$$

To express this as a percentage, simply multiply by 100.

Often the percent change will be given for some duration of time other than a year. For example, CPI data is released monthly and is reported as a monthly percent change. GDP, on the other hand, is reported every quarter (3 months) at an annual rate. In other words, they report the growth rate that would have been true for a year, had the quarterly rate held for a total of 4 quarters.

To compute the annual percent changes g^A given the quarterly growth g^Q the following formula can be used:

$$(1+g^Q)^4 = (1+g^A),$$

For monthly data, this becomes:

$$(1+g^M)^{12} = (1+g^A).$$

If the growth rate is small, and the number of periods is small, this will reduce to a useful approximation:

$$g^Q \times 4 \approx g^A, \text{ and}$$
$$g^M \times 12 \approx g^A.$$

Index

Data is often expressed as an index when the unit of the data is not important. For example, GDP is not an index because the current value gives an indication of the size of the economy. For example, GDP in the United States is approximately $9 trillion. CPI, on the other hand, is an index because we don't really care about the cost of the typical basket of goods by itself - we only really care about how much it changes from year to year.

Indexes are calculated using a base year, and all other values are stated relative to that base. For example, an index will always have the value of 100 in the base year, and in other years will have a value either higher or lower depending upon the path of the series. Any data can be converted to an index by doing the following:

1.   Pick a base year; and then
2.   Divide each value in the series by the value in the base year and multiply by 100.

Tip. The Ln trick

The natural logarithm (ln) provides a nice trick for calculating growth rates. For small growth rates the following is a useful approximation:

$$\%\Delta X_t = \ln X_t - \ln X_{t-1}.$$

This approximation becomes handy when we are looking at two or more series that are related by multiplication and that are growing over time.

For example, suppose that real GDP is growing by 3% per year, and that nominal GDP is growing at 5% per year. How fast is the deflator growing?

$Deflator_t = Nominal\ GDP_t / Real\ GDP_t,$
$ln\ (Deflator_t) = ln\ (Nominal\ GDP_t) - ln\ (Real\ GDP_t),$
$ln\ Deflator_t - ln\ Deflator_{t-1} = [ln\ Nominal_t - ln\ Real_t] - [ln\ Nominal_{t-1} - ln\ Real_{t-1}],$
$ln\ Deflator_t - ln\ Deflator_{t-1} = [ln\ Nominal_t - ln\ Nominal_{t-1}] - [ln\ Real_t - ln\ Real_{t-1}],$

$\%\Delta\ deflator = \%\Delta\ Nominal\ GDP - \%\Delta\ Real\ GDP.$

So the deflator is growing at 5% − 3 % = 2% rate.

This trick will be useful throughout the book.

PROBLEMS AND EXERCISES

Multiple Choice Questions

1. GDP can be measured by all of the following except:

    a. Total income paid to all factors of production
    b. Total value of final sales to consumers
    c. Total value added by firms
    d. Total expenditures by all firms

2. If real GDP increases at a faster rate than nominal GDP, we know that:

    a. The CPI is falling
    b. The CPI is increasing
    c. The Deflator is falling
    d. The Deflator is increasing

3. The GDP deflator differs from the CPI because

    a. The deflator uses a base year
    b. Each measures the prices of a different set of goods
    c. The CPI measures only goods
    d. The deflator does not adjust for quantity changes

4. Which of the following does not lead to a bias in the CPI?

    a. Substitution from more expensive goods to less expensive goods
    b. The introduction of new products
    c. Unmeasured differences in quality
    d. The use of a fixed basket of goods
    e. All of the above lead to a bias

5. Which of the following is included in the unemployment rate?

    a. Discouraged workers
    b. Retired people
    c. Employed people looking for a better job
    d. People who just entered the labor force, but who have not yet found jobs

6. Which of the following represents the largest component of GDP?

    a. Consumption
    b. Investment
    c. Government spending
    d. Net Exports

7.   The largest component of national income is:

   a.   Employee compensation
   b.   Proprietors' income
   c.   Profits
   d.   Net interest
   e.   Rent

8.   The PPI measures:

   a.   All prices excluding imports
   b.   All prices excluding services
   c.   Prices of goods and services typically purchased by firms
   d.   Only prices of heavy machinery

9.   A business cycles peak is the beginning of a(n):

   a.   Expansion
   b.   Recession
   c.   Inflation
   d.   Deflation

10.   The trade balance is necessarily in surplus if:

   a.   Exports exceed imports
   b.   Imports exceed exports
   c.   Capital inflows exceed outflows
   d.   Capital outflows exceed inflows

True/False/Uncertain

For each of the questions below, answer true, false, or uncertain. Explain your answer in each case.

1.   If a foreign company opens an auto plant in the U.S., then sales from that plant to consumers are added to GDP.

2.   A complete business cycle begins at a peak and ends in a trough.

3.   The trade surplus in the U.S. has been steadily increasing over time.

4.   The U.S. currently has a flexible exchange rate regime.

5.   The unemployed include everyone in the population who does not have a job.

Problems

1. Assume a hypothetical economy with the following production and prices.

    Quantity:

2000			2001	
Apples	Bananas		Apples	Bananas
10	10		12	15

    Price:

2000			2001	
Apples	Bananas		Apples	Bananas
$1	$2		$1	$2.20

    Assuming 2000 is used as the base year, find the values of

    a. Nominal GDP in 2000 and 2001
    b. Growth rate of Nominal GDP
    c. Real GDP in 2000 and 2001
    d. Growth rate of Real GDP
    e. GDP deflator in 2000 and 2001
    f. Rate of growth of prices as measured by the deflator from 2000 to 2001

2. Consider the following set of transactions.

    A fisherman catches a 30-pound tuna and sells it to a canning company for $30.

    The canning company then processes the tuna, puts it in 100 cans (which it purchased for $0.10 each) and sells them to a restaurant for 1$ a can.

    The restaurant then combines the 100 cans of tuna with 10 loaves of bread (which it purchased for 1$ a loaf), and sells 200 tuna sandwiches to customers at 3$ each.

    a. Calculate the value added for each of these three firms separately. Find the sum of the three.
    b. What is the contribution to GDP from these transactions as measured by the final value of goods and services produced?
    c. Should your answers to a and b be the same? Explain.

3. Use the following data to answer the questions below.

    The CPI was 82.4 in 1980 and 172.2 in 2000.
    The average price of a car was about $5,400 in 1980 and about $22,000 in 2000.

    a. What was the total percentage increase in prices between 1980 and 2000?

  b. What was the annual rate of inflation over this period?
  c. What was the total percentage increase in the price of a car between 1980 and 2000?
  d. If the 1980 price of a car were adjusted for inflation to 2000, how much would it cost?
  e. If the 2000 price of a car were adjusted for inflation to 1980, how much would it cost?
  f. Given these results, what can we say about the *relative* average price of a car?
  g. Why might your answer in *f* be misleading if we then made the claim that cars are more expensive today than in 1980?

4. Given the following numbers about the employment situation (June 2001, in millions):

Civilian labor force:	141,858
Employment:	135,864
Unemployment:	5,994
Not in labor force:	69,171

  Find:

  a. The unemployment rate.
  b. The employment rate.
  c. The labor force participation rate.

5. Suppose that:

  • Population (L) grows by 1% per year,
  • Nominal GDP grows at 6.5% per year,
  • The GDP deflator and the CPI grow at 3% per year, and
  • The nominal average hourly wage grows at 5.5% per year.

  Find the growth rates of

  a. Real GDP (Y)
  b. Real GDP per capita (Y/L)
  c. The real hourly average wage (W/P), where P is the price level, and W is the nominal wage.

Internet Exercises

1. The unemployment rate varies across states and across demographic groups. For the current year, find:

  a. The unemployment rate for the U.S.
  b. The unemployment rate for your state
  c. The unemployment rate for your age group
  d. The unemployment rate for your race
  e. The unemployment rate for your sex

  See http://stats.bls.gov.

2. Data/Graphing. For each year from 1960 to the present, find and graph over time

    a. Real GDP
    b. Total Population
    c. GDP per capita

    See http://www.bea.doc.gov/bea/dn1.htm.

3. Data/Graphing. For each year from 1960 to the present, find and graph over time

    a. Growth rate of real GDP
    b. Unemployment rate
    c. The change in the unemployment rate
    d. Inflation rate

    You may need to construct these series from the underlying data. Also, you will use this data in the next chapter, so keep it handy.

    In addition to the above web sites see: http://stats.bls.gov/cpihome.htm.

4. Visit the CPI home page at: http://stats.bls.gov/cpihome.htm.

    a. What is the "core CPI", and how does it differ from the CPI?
    b. What does CPI-U stand for?

5. Data. Find the following average prices for each of the following in 1970 and adjust for inflation. In addition, find the actual price in 1996.

	1970		1996
	Actual Price	Adjusted for inflation ($1996)	Actual price
Postage Stamp	_____	_____	_____
Car	_____	_____	_____
Gallon of Milk	_____	_____	_____
House	_____	_____	_____
Average Income	_____	_____	_____

    a. For which goods have the relative prices increased?

    b. As a fraction of income, what has happened to the cost of each of these goods?

    See http://www.inthe70s.com/prices.shtml; http://stats.bls.gov/cpihome.htm

6. The BLS adjusts many of its price numbers for improvements in quality. This is done by a method called hedonic pricing. Describe what quality measures are used to adjust prices for:

   a. DVD players
   b. Refrigerators
   c. College Textbooks
   d. College Tuition
   e. Microwave Ovens

   See http://stats.bls.gov/cpihome.htm

7. Who are the top trading partners for the U.S.? What do the top two countries have in common? Do you think that this pattern holds true for other countries?

   See http://www.census.gov/foreign-trade/www/

CHAPTER 3.
GRAPPLING WITH INFLATION, UNEMPLOYMENT AND GROWTH

OBJECTIVES

1. Discuss the costs of inflation.
2. Explain how inflation can be both grease and sand to an economy.
3. Explain why economists focus on the unemployment goal and why some unemployment is necessary.
4. Demonstrate the natural rate of unemployment by adjusting the standard demand and supply curves for labor for search costs and wage pressures.
5. Show the observed short-run relationship between inflation and unemployment using the Phillips Curve.

OVERVIEW

While the previous chapter introduced you to the various measures of the macroeconomy, this chapter discusses the *interpretation* of the central measures. The central question to keep in mind is a normative one – what level of inflation and unemployment should be chosen if we had perfect control over these variables? Towards this end, this chapter will examine the costs and benefits of various levels of inflation and unemployment. Unfortunately, policymakers are not able to control each of the three factors of inflation, unemployment, and growth independently, so the chapter begins to examine the relationship between inflation and unemployment and growth.

GOALS OF LOW INFLATION, LOW UNEMPLOYMENT, AND GROWTH

Policymakers often consider the unemployment and inflation consequences of their policies. There has been (and still is) much debate over which goal should be more important: for example should the Federal Reserve focus solely on keeping inflation at a low level, or should the Fed consider the unemployment and growth consequences of policy as well as inflation when making decisions? Congress has established that the Fed should aim to achieve both a satisfactory employment and inflation outcome. However, many have argued that the Fed cannot affect the natural rate of unemployment and should focus only on inflation.

To the extent that the two goals are in conflict (at least in the short-run), we must be able to weigh the consequences of pursuing one goal at the expense of the other. To guide policy, we would like to know the answers to two questions. First, what is an "ideal" level of inflation and unemployment for the economy? Second, how costly is having inflation or unemployment deviate from these ideal levels?

INFLATION AND POLICY

First, we need to dispel a myth. Inflation is *not* costly because goods and services are "more expensive." When we speak of inflation, we talk of a rise in the average level of prices – including people's wages, which is the price of an hour's worth of labor. So, when there is inflation, there is also a corresponding increase in people's dollar income.

The costs of inflation are subtler than this (incorrect) explanation and are investigated below.

Hint. Thinking about inflation

When you think about an economy where prices change from year to year, you should always think of the price change as containing two components - an "absolute" or "nominal" price change due to inflation, and a "relative" or "real" price change due to the good's price relative to other goods.

So if all prices in the economy, including the wage, were to double overnight, people would be able to afford the exact same amount of goods - and hence goods are not really "more expensive". If all the prices on goods and services were to double, but the wage were to remain constant, we would describe this as inflation coupled with a decline in the real wage. In other words, people would be upset by the decline in their wage relative to the other prices in the economy.

Redistribution

Inflation can cause some redistribution of resources. While not directly a "cost" of inflation since one persons loss is another's gain; the redistribution of resources can be an unwanted consequence.

Inflation can cause a redistribution of income from those who do not or cannot raise their prices to those who can and do raise their prices. In particular, we must consider the effects of anticipated versus unanticipated inflation and contracts.

Loans and labor contracts are examples of future payments that are written into contracts today. If both parties in a contract anticipate inflation correctly, then the contracts will take this into account. However, if inflation turns out to be other than what the two parties were expecting, then there will be an arbitrary distribution of wealth from one party to another.

In particular, if inflation is higher than expected, then the agreed-to payments will be worth less than was initially anticipated. In general, unexpected inflation benefits those who must make payments in the future. In the case of loan contracts, borrowers benefit from unexpected inflation, while lenders lose.

Note: Contracts could be indexed to inflation, that is, future payments could be automatically adjusted at the time of payment to reflect the rate of inflation. However, nominal contracts are the norm in countries with low inflation.

Costs of Inflation

Information and Uncertainty. Prices play an important role in the economy as they transmit information about production costs and the value of goods. The informational cost of inflation indicates that inflation may lead prices to contain less inflation than would be ideal. In particular, consumers will roughly know the relative price of goods they regularly consume. With high rates of inflation, consumers may not be able to completely store enough information about prices. The uncertainty cost of inflation comes from the fact that high inflation is often associated with variable inflation. If consumers are unsure about what inflation will be next year, it becomes very difficult to make good decisions today about what to consume today. This is a particular problem for businesses considering investment projects.

Institutional and Constitutional Costs. Economies with stable prices tend to develop institutions and conventions that depend on stable prices. If inflation were to increase, these conventions will break down, sometimes imposing costs on the economy. In addition, constitutional costs are born if high inflation erodes people's confidence in the government and the economy as a whole. High inflation may even destroy people's confidence in the entire monetary system and cause a reversion to a barter system.

Menu and Shoe-Leather Costs. The shoe-leather costs of inflation arise because people must be more diligent about managing their money in a high inflation environment. For example, when inflation is high, it is very costly to keep cash in your pocket, because the cash looses its value rapidly. You'd be better off keeping it in an interest bearing account at the bank. So when inflation is high, you may make frequent trips to the ATM machine - these wasted resources in time and other expenses represent a cost of inflation. The menu costs represent the cost that firms must bear when they are forced to change prices on menu, catalogues, and other ticked merchandise. The higher the rate of inflation, the more frequent firms will change their prices and the more they will have to spend for the changes.

Low Inflation: Grease or Sand?

The above costs of inflation would suggest the best level of inflation might be an inflation rate of zero. But is this really the case? Some economists argue that there may be some benefits from a low, but positive, rate of inflation.

One argument stems from the observation that firms are often reluctant to lower prices and people don't like to see their (nominal) wages decline. In any economy, relative prices should adjust to reflect changes in production costs and changes in demand; hence, some prices should be rising while others should be falling. If prices cannot fall, then some inflation may allow relative prices on some goods to fall without changing the posted price.

This may be particularly true of wages. People are reluctant to accept a lower wage. However, the economy depends on having relative wages in some industries and occupations rise and hence others' relative wages fall in order to achieve an efficient allocation of labor resources. Having some inflation may allow relative wages to decline more rapidly than otherwise.

Some inflation may thus allow the economy to operate more efficiently.

Note: Which raise would you choose?

If you were given a choice, which situation would you rather have?

    a) 5% wage raise, 10% inflation
    b) 2% raise, 7% inflation
    c) 5% pay cut, 0% inflation.

Most people will probably answer (a), even though each outcome is the same in terms of the real purchasing power of their wage. As a result, people might be more willing to accept a real wage cut when there is inflation in the economy.

UNEMPLOYMENT AND POLICY

Unemployment has personal and economy-wide costs. However, some unemployment is inevitable, and even beneficial.

Why is Some Unemployment Necessary?

The economy in any given year sees millions of people entering and exiting the labor market. In addition, there are a large number of jobs that are created and destroyed in any given year due to changes in technology and tastes. Since it often takes time to find a new job, some unemployment is necessary.

Flows In and Out of the Labor Market. The monthly flows into and out of employment is about 4% of the total level of employment. In addition, there are large flows between employment, unemployment, and the group of people not in the labor market.

Facts about the unemployed: Duration.

- Average: <3 months.
- Median: 5 weeks.
- 25% between 5 and 14 weeks
- 12.3% >6 months

Vacancies. While there are people who would like to have jobs but do not, there are also firms who would like to hire, but have not. The result is a job vacancy. Vacancies can arise if a firm expands its workforce or if a worker is separated from her job.

Labor Market as Matchmaker. A well functioning labor market will match the right people to the right jobs. Workers searching for jobs and firms looking to fill jobs each spend time and resources to find the right match. Workers have to send out resumes, go on interviews, etc. Firms must place ads, review resumes, and conduct interviews. The resulting friction will lead to some unemployment.

The Standard Supply and Demand Curves and the Dynamic Labor Market

The standard model of supply and demand in the market for labor often assumes that matches are made instantaneously. Under this assumption and if wages are flexible, then there would be no unemployment.

If we instead take into account that jobs are not instantly filled, and that job seekers cannot instantly enter into a new job, we can modify the standard supply and demand framework. The matched supply curve (S_M) shows how many workers actually find jobs at a given wage and is always to the left of the supply curve. Similarly, the matched demand curve (D_M) is the number of jobs filled at a given wage and is always to the left of the demand curve.

The intersection of the S_M and D_M shows the equilibrium level of employment and the equilibrium wage when taking search into account. The difference between this level of employment and the supply curve at this wage is the amount of frictional unemployment in the economy.

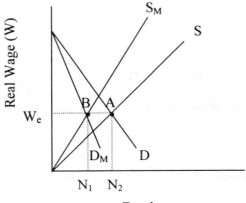

In addition, there may be some unemployment if the wage is pushed above the equilibrium wage. If this happens, it is called insider-outsider unemployment. Wage pressure from "insiders" – including unions and other employees, or from other sources such as a minimum wage – may cause this increase in the wage. In addition, efficiency wages may also push the wage above the equilibrium. Reduced turnover, finding the "right" people, and keeping morale high might be reasons why firms might wish to increase their wage above the equilibrium.

The Natural Rate of Unemployment

Frictional and insider-outsider unemployment combine to create a normal, or "natural," rate of unemployment. The natural rate can change for a number of reasons. Demographics, temp agencies that reduce the cost of matching, prison populations, union memberships may all affect the level of the natural rate. In addition, some argue that supply shocks may also affect the natural rate in the short-run. The natural rate has been estimated over the past 20 years to be anywhere between 4% and 6%. It is thought to have fallen towards the low end of the range in recent years.

Note: The term "natural" does not mean to imply that there is something good about this level of unemployment. Only that this is the level of unemployment that the economy tends to return to over time.

Cyclical Unemployment and Aggregate Coordination Failures

The actual rate of unemployment can fluctuate around its natural rate. In general, in recessions the unemployment rate rises, and during recessions, the unemployment rate will fall. The fluctuation in unemployment about the natural rate that results when real output is below potential is called cyclical unemployment. This kind of unemployment can arise due to coordination failures, which are problems that develop in an economy because of dynamic feedback between decision makers.

Costs of Cyclical Unemployment. Cyclical unemployment is seen as a problem for the economy because it represents lost output – the economy is not operating up to it's potential. Okun's law shows the relationship between unemployment and output.

> Okun's law: $\%\Delta Q = 3.5 - 2\,\Delta U.$

Using this equation, a 1-percentage point rise in unemployment will be associated with a 2% reduction in output growth. In the U.S., this translates into about $2,000 per household per year.

The Equity Costs of Unemployment

In addition to the macroeconomic costs of unemployment, individuals also face a cost from being unemployed. Behind the headline number of the unemployment rate is hidden different experiences by different demographic groups. For example, the unemployment rate for teenagers as well as Blacks and Hispanics tend to be much higher than the overall rate.

THE PHILLIPS CURVE

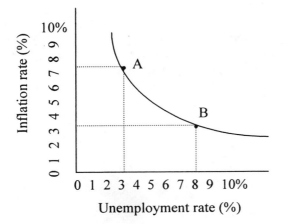

The Phillips curve is a representation of the short-run relationship between inflation and unemployment that has sometimes been observed in the economy. When inflation is high, unemployment tends to be low, and vice versa.

The curve became important because it represents a tradeoff, lower unemployment could only be achieved at the expense of higher inflation. The shape of the curve is important, because it tells us *how much* inflation must be endured to achieve a reduction in the unemployment rate.

The Phillips Curve in the United States

The Phillips curve, has had mixed success as a useful relationship. In the U.S. since the 1950s the curve has fit the data only in certain years - notable in the 60s and again in the late 80s. However, in other periods, there has been a much weaker relationship between inflation and unemployment - the late 70s saw high inflation and high unemployment, while the late 90s saw the reverse.

The Short-run and Long-run Phillips curve

To explain the empirical failure of a stable Phillips curve, economists have constructed a short-run curve as above, but then added a long-run Phillips curve. The long-run Phillips curve represents the idea that the economy will eventually return to the natural rate in the long-run. This curve is represented as a vertical line at the natural rate.

These two Phillips curves give us a rule of thumb, which is often used when thinking about policy: When the unemployment rate is below the natural rate, predict inflation to rise. When the unemployment rate is above its natural rate, predict inflation to fall.

POLICY PERSPECTIVE

When thinking about policy goals, we must be aware of the magnitude of the tradeoffs that we face in the economy. The Phillips curve combined with Okun's law can be stated in terms of a sacrifice ratio: the percentage of a year's real GDP that must be given up to permanently reduce annual inflation by 1 percentage point.

$$\text{GDP} \rightarrow (\text{Okun's law}) \rightarrow \text{Unemployment} \rightarrow (\text{Phillips curve}) \rightarrow \text{Inflation}$$

In the 1980's the sacrifice ratio was estimated to be 2.3. That is, a 1-percentage point reduction in inflation would "cost" 2.3% of real GDP -- over $200 Billion -- in the short-run.

On the other hand, we know that inflation has costs, and in the long-run it may decrease the growth rate of the economy. It is up to policymakers to make the judgments as to whether or not policies should be aimed at reducing inflation.

CONCLUSION

This chapter first looked at the costs (and benefits) of inflation and unemployment and then examined the relationship between the two as represented by the Phillips curve. While unstable at times, the Phillips curve represents an important short-run tradeoff between inflation and unemployment.

PROBLEMS AND EXERCISES

Multiple Choice Questions

1. Inflation is thought to be costly for each of the following reasons except:

    a. It distorts the information content of prices
    b. Inflation can weaken economic institutions
    c. Resources are expended by people managing their money
    d. Goods and services cost more

2. Lenders benefit from:

    a. High inflation
    b. Low inflation
    c. An unexpected rise in inflation
    d. An unexpected decline in inflation
    e. Low interest rates

3. The natural rate of unemployment:

    a. Is the optimal level of unemployment
    b. Does not change over time
    c. Is affected by the cost of matching jobs to workers
    d. Is always lower than the actual rate of unemployment

4. Cyclical unemployment can be a result of:

    a. Union membership
    b. Unemployment insurance
    c. Coordination failures
    d. Demographic changes

5. Okun's law is a relationship between:

    a. Inflation and output
    b. Output and unemployment
    c. Inflation and unemployment
    d. Inflation and nominal interest rates

6. The Phillips curve is a relationship between:

    a. Inflation and output
    b. Output and unemployment
    c. Inflation and unemployment
    d. Inflation and nominal interest rates

7. The sacrifice ratio measures the cost of reducing:

   a. Poverty
   b. Unemployment
   c. Inflation
   d. Interest rates
   e. The money supply

8. Labor market flows are greatest between:

   a. Employed and unemployed
   b. Employed and not in labor market
   c. Unemployed and not in labor market

9. Declines in the natural rate of unemployment since the 1980's have been contributed to by all of the following except:

   a. Increased prison population
   b. Growth in the temporary help industry
   c. Demographic shifts
   d. Decline in union memberships
   e. All of the above have contributed to some degree

10. Unemployment arising from wages that are above equilibrium is often called:

   a. Insider-outsider unemployment
   b. Frictional unemployment
   c. Matched unemployment
   d. Unnatural unemployment

True/False/Uncertain

For each of the questions below, answer true, false, or uncertain. Explain your answer in each case.

1. The average duration of unemployment spells is greater than the median duration.

2. Lower unemployment is always preferable to higher unemployment.

3. The short-run Phillips curve is vertical on the Price/Output graph.

4. Lower inflation will always lead to higher output growth.

5. The unemployment rate is similar across racial, gender, and age groups.

Problems

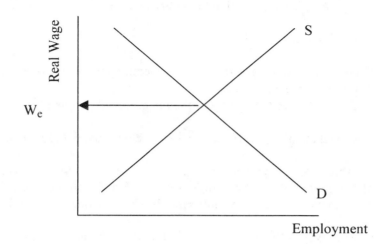

1. Using the standard supply and demand model for the labor market shown above, show the effect of a wage that is above the equilibrium wage. Be sure to label the amount of unemployment on the graph.

2. Using the labor market model shown above draw the matched supply and matched demand curves, and show the effects of a shift to the left of the demand curve on:

   a. Employment
   b. Natural Rate of Unemployment
   c. Wages

   What might cause this kind of shift?

3. Given a hypothetical Okun's rule of thumb and the Phillips Curve relation below, find the sacrifice ratio in this economy assuming we are currently at 4% inflation.

   Okun's relation: $\%\Delta Q = 3.5 - 2 \, \Delta U$.
   Phillips curve: Inflation $= 10 - 2 \, U$

4. The costs of inflation were discussed in the text; however, it is possible for countries to experience deflation (although it is rare). If inflation has costs, does deflation have benefits? Discuss possible costs and benefits of deflation. You may want to consider the following:

   a. Information costs
   b. Menu costs
   c. Shoe leather costs
   d. Institutional costs and constitutional costs
   e. Labor market functioning.

5.   [Hard]. Flow approach to the natural rate of unemployment.

Suppose that there are E people employed and U people unemployed, and that the labor force is given by $L = E + U$. Assume that the entire population is in the labor force.

Assume the following:

- Each year, a fixed fraction s of the employed people are separated from their job through quits, layoffs, etc.
- Each year, a fixed fraction f of the unemployed people find jobs.

This means that each year fU people become employed and sE people unemployed.

a.   Find the unemployment rate such that the flows into employment equal the flow out of employment. In other words, set $fU=sE$ and find the unemployment rate, $u = U/L$, as a function of s and f. (Hint: First divide both sides by L and note that $E = L - U$).

b.   In what way is the unemployment in part (a) the natural rate of unemployment?

c.   How will this rate change if the separation rate, s, increases?

d.   How will this rate change if the rate of job finds, f, increases?

e.   What policies might lead to changes in s and f?

Internet Exercises

1.   Data/Graphing. Using the data for inflation, unemployment, and growth that you found in the previous chapter, construct cross-plots of:

a.   Growth versus inflation (Phillips curve)
b.   Unemployment versus inflation
c.   Real GDP growth versus the change in unemployment (Okun's rule of thumb)

2.   You should now have a basic idea about the concepts of inflation, output and unemployment. The government faces a difficult task of having to go out and measure these quantities. How does the government gather this data?

a.   http://stats.bls.gov/cpshome.htm for the unemployment measurement.
b.   http://stats.bls.gov/cpihome.htm for the inflation rate.
c.   http://www.bea.doc.gov/bea/an1.htm for output measures.

3.   Find a news story that talks about the current unemployment rate and inflation. (See http://cnnfn.cnn.com in the "Economy" section.) What does the article suggest about whether or not the recent announcement was expected or not? Does it say anything about what policy has been in the past or will likely be in the future?

CHAPTER 4.
UNDERSTANDING POLICY FOR THE LONG-RUN AND THE SHORT-RUN

OBJECTIVES

1. Draw the circular flow model and explain the economic flows among the various sectors of the economy.
2. Define equilibrium for the economy using aggregate demand and aggregate supply concepts.
3. Define equilibrium for the economy using investment and savings concepts.
4. Describe the difference between long-run and short-run equilibriums.
5. Understand how fiscal policy affects the long-run and short-run equilibriums differently.

OVERVIEW

This chapter begins to examine the overall structure of the economy by introducing some basic issues surrounding long-run and short-run analysis. The long-run model will focus on the economy's production function and the factors of production, while the short-run model focuses on the role of aggregate demand and the impact on prices. While these models will be explored in more detail in the following chapters, the current chapter provides an introduction to some of the policy questions.

THE CIRCULAR FLOW MODEL OF THE MACROECONOMY

The circular flow diagram shows how the sectors of the economy interact and provides us with a way to define equilibrium for the short and long-run.

The diagram contains the main actors in the economy: firms, households, the government, and foreigners.

In addition, the diagram contains three main markets:

- Goods market: firms sell goods and services to households
- Factor market: households derive income by selling the factors of production – land, labor, and capital – to firms.
- Financial markets: channel flows of savings by households into investment by firms.

Flows between the actors can be either real, as in goods or services, or financial, as in money.

Firms and Production

Firms are assumed to produce the output of the economy. The quantity of output is determined via a production function:

$$Y = F(K, L)$$
$$Output = function\ of\ (capital,\ labor).$$

Hint: Black Box

Think of the production function as a "black box" where factors of production (K, L) go in one side and output (Y) comes out the other side. When you factor in technology, $Y = A \cdot F (K, L)$. The level of technology (A) determines the amount of Y that comes out for a given amount of inputs.

Assumptions about Production Processes

We assume that the production function has some characteristics:

1. Positive marginal product: output will increase as the quantity of inputs increases.
2. Constant returns to scale: output will increase by the same proportional increase in all inputs combined.
3. Diminishing marginal product: Output will increase by ever-smaller amounts as more of only one input is added, assuming all other inputs and the production process constant.

Given the production function and the assumptions above, we can describe how output would grow over time as the factors of production change. For now, we will assume that technology is exogenous.

Firms purchase the factors of production (labor and capital) from households. The purchase of labor is done by paying wages to workers. Firms pay for their capital either by renting the capital or by distributing profits to the owners of the capital – such as the firm's owner or shareholders.

The amount of capital that a firm uses will obviously depend on the cost of the capital. Firms increase the amount of capital they have on hand by investing. The greater is the cost of investing, the less they will do so. The cost of investment is given by the real interest rate - the higher the real interest rate, the higher will be the cost of borrowing money, and hence fewer investment projects will be undertaken.

Warning! When economists talk of saving and investing, we mean something very specific. It may be helpful to remember that (for the most part): *households save; firms invest.*

Households

Households receive income (Y) from supplying inputs to firms including their labor. They use this income to pay taxes (T), to consumer goods and services (C), and to save for the future (Sp). We define disposable income to be the income available after taxes. Private savings are what is left over after households consume.

> *Disposable income: (Y-T),*
> *Savings: Sp =(Y – T) - C = disposable income – consumption.*

Consumption is assumed to be related to disposable income as follows:

> *Consumption: C= C_0 + mpc(Y – T), with*
> *mpc = marginal propensity to consume.*

Hint. In the circular flow diagram the real flows must be equal in magnitude to the flows of the financial side. In addition, flows into and out of each group or market must be equal. You should convince yourself that the total output produced by firms in the economy ($Y = GDP$) is also equal to total income paid to households (Y).

Government

The government collects taxes (T) from households and spends some money on goods and services (G). Government savings is given by

$$S_g = T - G.$$

If S_g is negative, then we say the government is running a deficit.

Expansionary fiscal policy involves either lowering taxes (T) or raising government spending (G), or both. Contractionary policy does the opposite by either raising taxes, lowering spending or both.

Global Connections

The current account balance summarizes a country's trade in goods and services. A current account surplus occurs when the current account balance is positive which happens whenever exports exceed imports. A current account deficit occurs when the current account balance is negative (imports exceed exports).

The capital account summarizes flows of capital across borders. The capital account balance is the mirror image of the current account and is equal in magnitude to the negative of the current account balance. Foreign savings is equal to the capital account balance.

Net exports (X - M), Current account: = exports – imports,
Foreign Saving: S_f = capital account balance = – current account balance.

The Circular Flow, AS/AD Model of Equilibrium in the Economy

To describe equilibrium, we put together the components described in the previous sections. The aggregate supply/aggregate demand model (AS/AD) is a formal representation of production and expenditures, and their relationship to the price level. The AS curve represents production by firms, while the AD curve represents the expenditure side where households, firms, the government, and foreigners purchase goods and services from firms.

Warning! While the AS and AD curves we will draw in this section and following chapters will look much like supply and demand curves form your microeconomics course, they have very different interpretations. The AS curve does not represent marginal cost; and the AD curve does not represent individuals' valuation of goods and services.

Aggregate demand is a function of the price level and is lower when the price level is higher (negative slope).

Aggregate demand:

$$AD = C + I + G + (X - M).$$

The aggregate supply shows how the price level and output responds to changes in aggregate demand. The shape of the AS curve depends on whether we are talking about the short-run or the long-run.

Aggregate supply:

$$AS = Y.$$

In the short-run, we will assume that prices are fixed; hence, the short-run AS curve is horizontal. This means that a shift in the aggregate demand curve will cause an equal change in equilibrium output and no price change in the short-run.

In the long-run, output is given by the level of potential output; hence, the long-run AS curve is vertical. This means that a shift in the aggregate demand curve will cause a change in prices, and no change in output in the long-run.

In equilibrium:

$$AS = AD,$$
$$Y = C + I + G + (X - M)$$

This is equivalent to saying savings ($S = S_p + S_g + S_f$) equals investment (I).

LONG-RUN VS. SHORT-RUN EQUILIBRIUM

Policy will often have different effect in the long-run than in the short-run. In the AS/AD model, the difference between the two time horizons is the response of prices to changes in demand. In the short-run prices are fixed through custom, contracts, or business practices. In the long-run, prices are free to adjust, and output returns to potential.

In the Short-Run, Demand Rules

Aggregate demand is given by total expenditures: $C + I + G + (X - M)$. In the short-run changes in any one of these factors will shift the AD curve and will lead to an equal increase in equilibrium output. Hansen's Law summarizes: in the short-run demand creates its own supply.

In the Long-Run, Supply Rules

In the long-run, output is given simply by potential output and is determined by capital, labor, and technology via the production function. Hence, any shift in aggregate demand will lead only to a price change with no corresponding change in output. Say's Law summarizes: in the long-run, supply creates it's own demand.

Quick exercise: Show what happens to the equilibrium price level and real output in the long-run and the short-run for an outward shift in AD and an inward shift in AD.

The Equality of Saving and Investment

In the short-run, output is driven by investment: I → Y → C, S.

An increase in investment leads to an increase in output, and since output is equal to income, consumption and savings increase as well.

If the private savings rate were to increase, this would mean a corresponding decrease in consumption, and hence a decline in AD and equilibrium output.

In the long-run, savings drives output:

$$S \rightarrow I \rightarrow K \rightarrow Y$$

An increase in savings means that there is more money available for firms to invest. The greater investment leads to more capital and hence more output via the production function.

We see that a change in the savings rate might have very different impacts on output in the economy in the short-run and the long-run.

Crowding Out

In the long-run, since output is fixed, an increase in government spending with no change in taxes will necessarily lead to a decline in investment. This is because government savings has declined (and private savings has not changed) and because investment equals savings. This is called crowing out because government expenditures take the place of private investment.

In the short-run, since output may fluctuate, an increase in government spending will increase output and thus may increase private savings. Crowding out may or may not happen in this case.

POLICY PERSPECTIVE: CHOOSING BETWEEN THE SHORT-RUN AND THE LONG-RUN FRAMEWORKS

If the economy is below potential, then the short-run framework may be more appropriate in determining policy. In this case, policy should focus on returning the economy to its potential. If the economy is operating at potential, then it may be best to focus on long-run framework to determine policy. However, this question is the subject of debate since the economy is always simultaneously in a short-run and some other long-run. The long-run situation may in principle depend upon the short-run outcome.

CONCLUSION

This chapter has introduced you to some of the basic relationships used to explain the level of output and the level of prices in the economy. The circular flow diagram provides a basic picture of the main actors and markets in the macroeconomy. In equilibrium, total output equals total expenditure and investment equals savings. In the short-run aggregate demand determines output, while in the long-run the production function determines the level of potential and actual output.

The following chapters will expand on these ideas. The long-run model presented in the next three chapters will focus on the production function and capital accumulation through investment. The short-run model presented in Chapters 8-11 will expand upon the AS/AD models and will focus on the role of aggregate demand in determining output.

PROBLEMS AND EXERCISES

Multiple Choice Questions

1. Which of the following is NOT included in the circular flow diagram of the economy?

    a. Goods market
    b. Factor markets
    c. Financial markets
    d. Households
    e. All of the above are included

2. The aggregate production function relates:

    a. Prices of factors to output
    b. Output to the quantity of factors of production
    c. Employment to the quantity of capital
    d. Consumption to income

3. The assumption that if one factor doubles, output will less than double is called:

    a. Positive marginal product
    b. Diminishing marginal product
    c. Decreasing returns to scale
    d. Constant returns to scale

4. The assumption that if all factors double, output will exactly double is called:

    a. Positive marginal product
    b. Diminishing marginal product
    c. Decreasing returns to scale
    d. Constant returns to scale

5. The level of investment varies _____ with the _____ interest rate.

    a. Positively; real
    b. Positively; nominal
    c. Negatively; real
    d. Negatively; nominal

6. Hansen's Law says that in the short-run, output is determined primarily by:

    a. Aggregate supply
    b. Aggregate demand
    c. Potential output
    d. Both a. and c.

7. Say's Law says that in the long-run, output is determined primarily by:

   a. Aggregate supply
   b. Aggregate demand
   c. Potential output
   d. Both a. and c.

8. In the long-run, an increase in spending with no change in taxes will lead to:

   a. Higher output
   b. Greater consumption
   c. Lower investment
   d. All of the Above

9. The difference between gross and net investment is:

   a. Depreciation
   b. Savings
   c. Profits
   d. Foreign savings
   e. Budget deficit

10. The current account balance measures _____; and the capital account balance measures _____.

    a. Exports less imports; capital inflows less capital outflows
    b. Capital inflows less capital outflows; exports less imports
    c. Imports less exports; capital inflows less capital outflows
    d. Capital outflows less capital inflows; exports less imports

True/False/Uncertain

For each of the questions below, answer true, false, or uncertain. Explain your answer in each case.

1. Investment must equal government savings plus private savings.
   Investment equals All i in the economy

2. Exports cannot exceed production. *production is the maximum amount an economy can produce*

3. In the long-run an increase in government spending will have no impact on investment.
   Increase in government spending lower the amount of government investment

4. In the short-run an increase in government spending will have no impact on private savings.
   Increases in government spending reduce private saving if they ink

5. Constant returns to scale implies that there are diminishing marginal returns, if there is more than one factor of production and all factors have positive marginal product.
   Constant return to scale means all factors have a impact k equally so therefore one acting alone create marginal returns

Problems

1. Define $y = Y/L$ and $k = K/L$. Graph each of the following production functions:

    a. $y = 2k$
    b. $y = k^{0.5}$
    c. $y = k^2$

    Which of these functions has constant returns to scale? Which of these functions has diminishing marginal product of capital?

2. Consider the following Cobb-Douglas production function:

    $$Y = K^a L^{(1-a)}, \text{ where } 0 < a < 1.$$

    a. Does this function have constant returns to scale?
    b. Divide both sides of this equation to get a relation between $y (= Y/L)$ and $k (= K/L)$ that does not depend on L.
    c. [More difficult] Show that in general any function $Y = F(K, L)$ that has constant returns to scale can be written as another function $y = f(k)$.

3. For each of the following production functions, determine which have i) constant returns to scale, ii) diminishing marginal product of capital, and iii) diminishing marginal returns to labor.

    a. $Y = L K$
    b. $Y = L + K$
    c. $Y = 2L + K$
    d. $Y = L^{0.5} K^{0.5}$
    e. $Y = L^{0.7} K^{0.3}$
    f. $Y = L^{0.7} K$
    g. $Y = L^{1.5} K^{0.3}$

4. Given a consumption function $C = 100 + 0.9 Y$, find the marginal propensity to save (assume taxes equals zero). In other words, find an equation $S^p = S_0 + mps\, Y$ and find the value of *mps*.

    Given this result, what do you think is the general rule that relates *mpc* and *mps*?

5. Assume:

    GDP is $10 Trillion,
    Personal disposable income is $9 trillion
    Consumption is $7 trillion
    Trade deficit is 0.
    Government budget deficit is $0.5 billion.

    Find:
    a. Private Savings (S_p)
    b. Investment (I)
    c. Government spending (G)

6. Use the AS/AD model to show the short-run and long-run effects on equilibrium output and prices of the following shocks:

   a. An increase in government spending
   b. A decline in investment

Internet Exercises

1. Data/Graphing. Find the level of imports and exports from 1960 to the present. Use this data to construct the trade deficit for each year and graph.

   See http://www.bea.doc.gov/bea/di1.htm.

2. Is a trade deficit good or bad for the economy? Try to find an economic commentary or news story that arguing each side of the debate.

3. Data/graphing. Find data on real GDP, annual consumption, investment, government spending, and net exports from 1929 to the present. Graph the growth rate of each of these series over time. Do any of the components tend to fluctuate more than the others? Which component seems to be the most stable? The most variable?

   Files that can be downloaded into a spreadsheet can be found at:
   http://www.bea.doc.gov/bea/dn/nipaweb/ (Table 1.2)

CHAPTER 5.
NEOCLASSICAL GROWTH MODEL

OBJECTIVES

1. Briefly summarize the history of growth.
2. Summarize the implications of the Solow growth model.
3. Explain the effect of changes in savings rate, population growth, and shifts in technology in the Solow growth model.
4. Describe the policy implications of the Solow growth model.
5. State the shortcomings of the Solow growth model.

OVERVIEW

The Solow growth model (and variations) is the most common framework with which to analyze long-run growth in economies. Countries have had very different growth experience both across time and across nations. Small differences in growth rates can easily compound over time to produce large differences in standards of living. Therefore, understanding what drives growth is vitally important. The Solow growth model may seem complex initially, but there are basically four parts:

1. A production function with certain characteristics,
2. An assumption about savings behavior and population growth,
3. A description of how capital changes over time, and
4. The concept of steady state equilibrium.

Once you learn these pieces and a couple of tricks, it is easy to use the Solow model to analyze a wide variety of phenomenon. As we go along, we will examine the equilibrium outcome of the economy as well as the transition to the equilibrium.

A VERY BRIEF HISTORY OF GROWTH

Until the early 1800s, the world's economies were characterized by very low levels of growth: about 0.07% per year. Since then, and starting with the industrial revolution, growth has accelerated and has averaged about 1.2% per year. Growth rates tend to vary from country to country and from decade to decade. Growth was most rapid for many developed countries, including the U.S., in the period after World War II from 1950 to the early 1970's. Since then growth has slowed for most countries.

GROWTH, MARKETS, AND ECONOMIES

While no one factor appears to be the key to growth, there are several types of policies that tend to promote growth.

1. Maintain stable political, social, and market environments that give individuals freedom to operate. This allows individual specialization to create a well-working economy.

2. Save and invest to build up the capital stock. Production requires capital, and thus savings are needed to increase the capital stock and hence output.

3. Educate the people in society. Human capital formation is necessary to create a productive economy and to develop new technology.

THE SOLOW GROWTH MODEL

As mentioned above the Solow growth model consists of several pieces. The central focus is on supply — the production function and the factor of production. Since the Solow model is a description of the long-run, we ignore the components of aggregate demand and assume that all factors in the economy are fully employed.

The Production Function

The production function is assumed to have constant returns to scale, and diminishing marginal product for both capital and labor.

$Y = A \cdot F (K, L)$
Output = technology $\cdot$ F (capital, labor)

To make things easier, we focus on output and capital per person: $y = Y/L$, and $k = K/L$. Since the production function has constant returns to scale, we can write the production function as $y = A \cdot f(k)$.

Key assumptions: The production function has diminishing marginal product and constant returns to scale. Technology is exogenous.

Note: Writing the production function in per capita terms makes the model's math and graphical analysis easier to handle. In addition, when we talk about growth, what we care about is really output per person. For example, suppose that country X had a greater GDP than country Z. You wouldn't be able to tell which country was economically better off without knowing the population of each country.

Forces that Increase Capital

The capital stock increases as firms invest. We assume that people save a fixed fraction v of their income. Since investment equals savings, $I = S = vY$. Since output is given by the production function we know that

$i = I/L = v(Y)/L = v (Y/L) = v [A \cdot f(k)]$

Key assumption: Savings, and hence investment, is a fixed fraction of output. The savings rate is exogenous.

Forces that Reduce Capital

While investment adds to the capital stock, there are other forces that will tend to decrease the capital stock.

Depreciation represents the wear and tear on capital from the production process. We assume that in any given year the rate of depreciation is a constant, d, that is, each year the capital stock declines by a fraction d.

In addition, for a fixed capital stock, population growth will lower the amount of capital per worker. If the level of capital is constant, then a 2 percent growth in population will lead to a 2 percent reduction in the amount of capital per person. The population growth rate, n, is assumed to be constant.

Key assumption: Population growth and the depreciation rate are both constant and exogenous.

Trick (Reminder)
Remember from the previous chapter the ln trick. We are interested in size of the change in K/L. Each year, if there is no investment, we have a change in capital of $\%\Delta K = -d$, and an increase in population of $\%\Delta L = n$.

So

$$
\begin{aligned}
\%\Delta k \quad &= \%\Delta(K/L) \\
&= ln\,(K/L)_t - ln(K/L)_{t-1} \\
&= ln\,K_t - ln\,L_t - (ln\,K_{t-1} - ln\,L_{t-1}) \\
&= ln\,K_t - ln\,k_{t-1} - (ln\,L_t - ln\,L_{t-1}) \\
&= \%\Delta(K) - \%\Delta(L) \\
&= -d - n \\
&= -(d + n).
\end{aligned}
$$

Balanced Growth Investment

So far the factors that affect capital are:

- Investment, which tends to increase capital, and
- Depreciation and population growth, which tend to decrease capital.

When the two forces are equal, capital per person is constant. This occurs when

$$i = (n + d)\,k.$$

This equation can be graphed as a line with slope *(n+d)*.

Equilibrium in the Solow Growth Model

The steady-state equilibrium is a dynamic equilibrium in which central variables are unchanging, and is given by the intersection of the balanced growth investment line, $i = (n+d)\,k$, and investment function, $i = s = v\,f(k)$.

At this point, capital per person and output per person are constant. If the population is growing, then capital and output are both growing at the rate of population growth in the steady-state equilibrium.

In the model, if the economy's capital stock is not equal to the equilibrium, the level of capital will adjust to bring it into equilibrium.

The following graph of output, savings, and depreciation summarizes equilibrium in the Solow growth model.

Solow Growth Model:

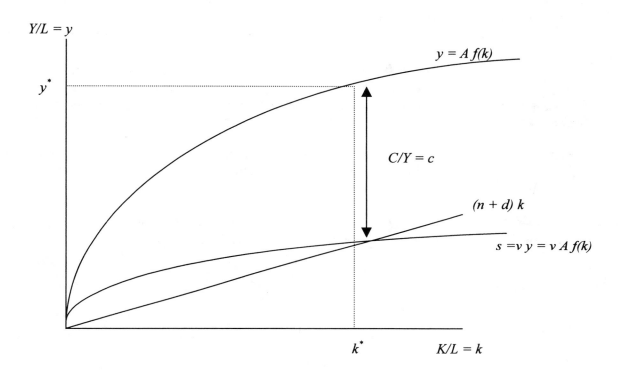

Hint. Why do we need a new definition of equilibrium called the steady state?

In models you've seen before, equilibrium involved reaching a point where there was no pressure for any of the variables to change. In the steady state equilibrium, many of the variables are changing over time – output, capital, and population are all growing. Even though the values are changing over time, it is still equilibrium, because each of these variables settles down to an equilibrium *growth rate*; and once at the steady state equilibrium, there is no tendency to deviate from the equilibrium growth rate.

IMPLICATIONS OF THE SOLOW GROWTH MODEL

The Solow growth model takes as given the savings rate, the depreciation rate, the rate of population growth, and the level of technology. We can thus use the model to find the effect of a change in any of these variables on the steady state

---

Warning! When using the Solow model (and other growth models) you will need to be very careful to distinguish between the *level* of output versus the *growth rate* output. In addition, you should distinguish between temporary effects in the transition to a new steady state versus permanent effects of locating the new steady state. Many of the factors below will permanently affect the equilibrium level output, but will have only a temporary effect on the growth rate of output.

Advisory! It is highly recommended that you learn how to derive the results below from Solow model rather than just memorizing the results.

An increase in the Savings Rate

A higher savings rate will lead to a higher level of capital per person and a higher level of income per person, but it will not lead to persistent growth per person. In the steady state, the economy will grow at the rate of population growth. Income per person does not grow in the steady state.

A higher savings rate, while increasing output per person, may not necessarily increase *consumption* per person. A change in the savings rate may increase or decrease consumption depending upon the Golden Rule level of savings.

A Change in the Population Growth or the Rate of Depreciation

A rise in population growth leads to a permanently higher growth rate in total output, but lower output per person.

A rise in the rate of depreciation doesn't change the growth rate in total output, but does lead to lower output per person.

A change in population growth or depreciation does not lead to a permanent change in the growth rate of output per person.

A Change in Technological Progress

So far, there has been no way to create a sustained increase in the growth rate of output per person.

A one-time technological innovation will raise output (and income) per person, but will not lead to a permanently higher growth rate in output per person. In the steady state, total output will resume growing at the rate of population growth.

To achieve a permanently higher rate of growth, the technological innovation must continue every year.

CONCLUSIONS ABOUT SAVINGS, POPULATION GROWTH AND TECHNOLOGICAL INNOVATION

The intuition of the Solow model is as follows: As output and capital increases, so too does the total amount of depreciation. Since the production function has diminishing returns, it takes more and more capital to increase output. Eventually, the depreciation ends up absorbing most of the investment, and there is none left over to increase the capital stock.

The steady state is a balance between depreciation and population growth pushing capital down, and investment, which equals savings, pushing capital up. When these forces balance, the economy is in steady state equilibrium.

While changes in savings rates, population growth, depreciation, and one-time technology changes may change the equilibrium level of output per person and *temporarily* affect the growth rate of output per person; none of these factors will lead to a *permanent* change in the growth rate of output per person.

POLICY PERSPECTIVE: INCENTIVES FOR SAVINGS AND INVESTMENT

The prime candidate for a policy tool to encourage long-run growth appears to be savings. The population growth rate and the depreciation rate are both as hard to influence as a policy maker.

The Solow model, however, indicates that a higher savings rate will lead to higher output per person, but will not lead to permanently higher growth rates in output per person. So, policies to encourage savings may only have temporary effects. (In addition, a higher savings rate may not lead to higher consumption. See Q&A on the Golden Rule.)

Incentives for Saving

Tax incentives may be used to encourage savings. A consumption-based tax rather than an income tax will reward savings. Individual Retirement Accounts (IRAs) and other tax preferred retirement plans aim to increase the savings rate. Theory and evidence on the effectiveness of savings incentives is mixed.

Tax Incentives for Investment

A second set of policies to encourage growth includes tax incentives for investment. Often investment by firms allows a reduction of their tax burdens. Tax write-offs for depreciation of capital also encourage investment. The government may also give a tax credit for investment as well.

CONCLUSION

The Solow growth model provides a starting point for understanding what factors do (and do not) affect growth. We found that the exogenous variables will lead to a change in the level of output per person, but only a temporary change in the growth rate of output per person. In the Solow model, continuous change in technology appears to be the only way to get sustained economic growth per person. The next chapter will investigate some shortcomings of the Solow model, and will examine in more detail the role of technology.

PROBLEMS AND EXERCISES

Multiple Choice Questions

1. Approximately when did growth in the world's economies begin to rise above very low levels of growth?

    a. Early 1600s
    b. Early 1700s
    c. Early 1800s
    d. Early 1900s

2. According to the Solow growth model, what explains the growth of technology in the economy?

    a. Capital
    b. Labor
    c. Output
    d. None of the above, technology is exogenous

3. In the growth model, _____ adds to capital per person, while _____ and _____ tend to decrease capital per person.

    a. Technology; population growth; earthquakes
    b. Investment; depreciation; population growth
    c. Savings; budget deficits; imports
    d. Savings; trade balance; population growth

4. Which of the following factors is NOT *assumed* to be constant over time in the Solow growth model?

    a. Population growth
    b. Savings rate
    c. Capital stock
    d. Depreciation rate

5. Balanced growth investment is achieved when:

    a. Output equals capital depreciation: $Y = d\,K$
    b. Savings equals investment: $s = i$
    c. Per capital investment equals depreciation rate plus population growth rate times the capital stock: $i = (d + n)\,k$
    d. Output growth equals zero

6. An increase in the savings rate will lead to:

    a. An increase in the rate of output growth in the short-run
    b. An increase in the rate of output growth in the long-run
    c. Both a and b
    d. None of the above

7. A one-time increase in technology will lead to:

    a. An increase in the rate of output growth in the short-run
    b. An increase in the rate of output growth in the long-run
    c. Both a and b
    d. None of the above

8. According to the Solow growth model, if there is no increase in technology, the steady-state level of growth in output will equal:

    a. 4%
    b. The rate of depreciation
    c. The rate of population growth
    d. Zero.

9. According to the Solow growth model, sustained growth in the Solow growth in per capita output model can only come from:

    a. High levels of investment
    b. High savings rates
    c. Persistent technological innovation
    d. No depreciation
    e. All of the above

10. According to the Solow growth model, output per person is determined by:

    a. Technology
    b. The savings rate
    c. Depreciation
    d. Population growth
    e. All of the above

True/False/Uncertain

For each of the questions below, answer true, false, or uncertain. Explain your answer in each case.

Hint: For growth questions, you need to distinguish carefully among output (Y), output per capita (y), the rate of growth of output (%ΔY), and the rate of growth of output per capita (%Δy).

1. A greater savings rate is a good way to increase the long-run growth rate in the economy.

2. A greater savings rate will increase the level of output in the economy.

3. A greater savings rate will increase the level of consumption in the economy.

4. In steady state, if there is no technology growth, output and capital grow at the same rate.

5. An increase in the population growth rate will lead to a long-term increase in the rate of output growth, but a decrease in the level of output per person.

Problems

1. Use the Solow growth model graph to find the effects of each of the following changes. In each case be sure to say what happens to output per person in the short-run as well as in the new steady state. In addition, be sure to distinguish between what happens to the level of per-capita output as well as the growth rate. Assume that the economy is initially in steady state equilibrium.

   Also, explain in words why the level of output has changed (if indeed it has).

   a. Increase in the savings rate
   b. Decrease in the depreciation rate
   c. Increase in population growth rate
   d. One time increase in technology
   e. An earthquake causes the capital stock to fall by 50%

2. Suppose that output is determined by the production function $Y = K^{0.5}L^{0.5}$. Population growth is 1%, the depreciation rate is 2%, and the savings rate is 12%.

   a. Find the level of per capital output as a function of per capital labor.
   b. Find the steady state level of capital per person.
   c. Find the steady state level of output per person.
   d. What is the growth rate of output?

3. Convergence. Consider two countries are similar in every way except that one has twice the capital stock as the other. Assume the country with the higher level of capital has reached the steady state.

   a. On a Solow growth model graph, show the level of output in each country.
   b. Also show the level of investment per person in each country.
   c. At their current level of capital, show on the graph how capital per person would shrink if there were no investment.
   d. Show the level of net investment on the graph (b minus c).
   e. Which country will be growing faster in the short-run?
   f. Which country will grow faster after they reach the steady state?

4. Consider two countries are similar in every way except that one has a higher level of technology the capital stock as the other. Assume that the country with a lower level of technology has reached the steady state.

   a. On a Solow growth model graph, show the level of output in each country.
   b. Also show the level of investment per person in each country.
   c. At their current level of capital, show on the graph how capital per person would shrink if there were no investment.
   d. Show the level of net investment on the graph (b minus c).
   e. Which country will be growing faster in the short-run?

f.   Which country will grow faster after they reach the steady state?

5.   [Advanced] The Golden Rule level of savings is that savings rate for which consumption is maximized.

   a.   On the Solow growth model diagram, show the steady state level of per capita consumption c. Note that

$$C = C/L = (Y\text{-}S)/L = y - s$$

   b.   What could consumption per person be if the savings rate were extremely close to 1? Extremely close to zero? What does this imply about an optimal savings rate?

   Assume a production function:

   $Y = K^a L^{(1-a)}$, where $0 < a < 1$.

   c.   Divide both sides of this equation to get a relation between y ($= Y/L$) and k ($= K/L$).

   Assume population growth is zero and the depreciation rate is d.
   Note that this implies that in steady state savings equals depreciations: $s = d\,k$

   d.   Use this fact to find the steady state level of consumption per person as a function of the steady state level of capital k^{SS}, and the other parameters (a and d).

   e.   Use calculus to find the level of k^{SS} that maximizes consumption by setting $\delta c/\delta k^{SS}=0$.

   f.   Use this result to find the savings rate that will achieve this level of steady state capital. (Hint: remember that $s = v\,Y$)

Internet Exercises

1.   Data/Graphing. The Solow growth models focused on the role of savings and investment in determining output.

   a.   Find and graph the personal savings rate (as a percentage of disposable income) from 1960 to the present.
   b.   Find data on real GDP and investment from 1960 to the present. Graph the investment to GDP ratio (I/Y).
   c.   Compare the graphs in part (a) and part (b): do the data series tend to move together?
   d.   Why might the two series not match perfectly?

   See: http://www.bea.doc.gov/bea/dn1.htm.

CHAPTER 6.
BEYOND THE SOLOW GROWTH MODEL

OBJECTIVES

1. Give three reasons why it is important to go beyond the simple Solow growth model.
2. Describe the two ways that economists have gone beyond the simple Solow growth model.
3. Explain how the process by which technology is produced is central to new growth theory.
4. Describe the different policy recommendations of the Solow growth model and new growth theory.
5. Explain how the ideas of Adam Smith and Joseph Schumpeter are related to the ideas in new growth theory.

OVERVIEW

While the Solow growth model is a useful starting point for examining growth, there are several reasons why we might want to expand on the model or go in a different direction. First, while the Solow model emphasizes savings and investment, there are other factors that have been found to play an important role in explaining different growth experiences across countries. Second, the role that technology plays in the model can be expanded to gain greater insight into the growth process.

Throughout this chapter it will be useful to think about whether the Solow framework can simply be modified to take into account empirical and theoretical problems, or if we instead need to abandon the entire framework.

THREE REASONS TO GO BEYOND THE SOLOW GROWTH MODEL

1. The Solow growth model doesn't explain two important empirical observations: growth rates have tended to accelerate over the past 180 years, and poor countries aren't catching up to rich countries.
2. Sometimes saving and investing – the policy prescriptions of the Solow model – do not lead to higher income per person.
3. Technological innovation accounts for much of the growth in developed economies, but the Solow growth model doesn't explain where that technological innovation comes from, or how to encourage it.

The first two reasons are empirical, that is, the theory doesn't match the evidence. The final reason is theoretical – if technology is so important to the growth process, we should be able to do better than simply taking the level of technology as given.

Fitting the Facts
The Solow model predicts (1) that growth rates would decline over time as economies approach their steady states; and (2) that poor countries would grow faster than rich countries. The second prediction is called convergence. The empirical evidence shows that neither of these predictions has fared very well.

A second set of predictions hinges on the role of savings and investing. In the Solow model, an increase in savings would lead to a higher level of per capita income. Empirically, this relation between savings and income is not very strong.

Technology as a Residual

According to the growth accounting formula for the U.S.:

$$\%\Delta Y = \%\Delta A + 0.3\%\Delta K + 0.7\%\Delta L.$$

We find that a large fraction of output growth is a result of technological progress. The technology component is called the Solow Residual because it measures the contribution of technological progress to growth after measurable factors are accounted for.

One study found that technology accounted for 35% of output growth in the U.S. economy. In the Solow growth model, technology is taken as exogenous – the model does not explain anything about how technology might increase over time. So to the extent that we want to explain growth, the Solow model leaves out an important component.

MOVING BEYOND THE SIMPLE SOLOW GROWTH MODEL

There are two basic approaches to modifying a theory that has problems: expand the basic model, or develop a new framework. The efforts to expand the Solow model have tried to incorporate other factors to match better the empirical regularities that the Solow model missed. "New growth theory" represents a larger change in that it focuses much more on the role of technology in driving growth.

Expanding the Solow Growth Model

As mentioned above, the Solow growth model predicts that poorer countries will converge on income levels to richer countries. A less restrictive prediction is called conditional convergence, which is the prediction that incomes per person for economies *with similar attributes* will eventually become equal. There is some (mixed) evidence to support this prediction.

There are many reasons why countries might not converge. Three possible explanations include:

1. Differences across countries in the quality of the labor force through educational differences,
2. Differences across countries in economic and political institutions, and resulting social capital differences, and
3. Increasing returns to scale in the production function leading rich countries to get richer faster than poor countries.

A growth model that is expanded in any of these directions give new options to policymakers.

New Growth Theory

A more extensive reworking of the Solow growth model, often called new growth theory, focuses on the production of technology. The determinants of technology are analyzed and brought into these models. Technology is thus endogenous in these models, and often leads to a greater emphasis on increasing returns to scale and a reduction of the emphasis on diminishing marginal returns to capital. The next section will focus on the role of technology.

DETERMINANTS OF TECHNOLOGICAL INNOVATION

Suppose we had a production function for technology:

$T = f(K, L, T, E)$,
Technology = f (Capital, Labor, Technology, Environment).

Capital and labor in this case refer the amount of resources devoted to research and development of new technology. Technology is also an important determinant of technology production – computers are often used to design new and faster computers.

Technology can be general purpose in that it affects all aspects of production, or it can be more specific affecting only a small range of production. In addition, technology may take some time to diffuse throughout the economy. There may also be an aspect of learning by doing: as one does something, one becomes better at it.

Agglomeration effects are the concentration of firms with like production in a geographic area. The physical closeness of these firms may increase the transmission of new technologies and foster new innovations.

Each of these factors can lead to a positive feedback loop in the production of technology. This then leads to increasing returns to scale in the production of total output. In this case, we would not necessarily predict countries would converge over time.

The economic environment can be important in determining technology production. Government stability, protection of property rights, openness to trade, and enforcement of patent and copyright laws may encourage innovation. Patents – legal protection that gives the holder a monopoly right to an idea or a product – can increase the incentive to innovate, and to devote resources to research and development. To the extent that there is a public good aspect to technology, the government may wish to encourage research, even at the expense of having a monopoly producer.

IDENTIFYING THE CAUSES OF TECHNOLOGICAL DEVELOPMENT

It is hard to generalize from case studies the main factors that influence technological development. Path dependency – the idea that the history of an innovation's development matters – may play an important role. Technological development, in general, is a complicated process and hard to capture in an economic model.

NOT-SO-NEW GROWTH THEORY

Many of the ideas in new growth theory have been around for a long time. The role of specialization and increasing returns have been around since at least Adam Smith.

Shumpeter emphasized the role of the entrepreneur. He argued that individuals who see opportunities in the economy, take risks, and innovate are largely responsible for major technological changes and move the economy forward. In Shumpeter's vision of the economy, innovations by entrepreneurs create great booms, and recessions serve a useful purpose in that they weed out less useful innovations.

POLICY PERSPECTIVE: POLICIES TO AFFECT GROWTH

The importance of technology suggests that convergence may not be a necessary consequence of growth models. In addition, it opens the doors for policymakers to have a greater influence on long-run growth.

The chapter examined several policies that may affect growth to a greater or lesser extent.

- Reduce protectionism
- Establish private enterprise zones
- Lower Tax Rates
- Privatize
- Have an industrial policy

CONCLUSION

The models used to analyze growth are far from perfect. They should be used as a guide and a launching point to begin thinking about the various factors that affect growth. New growth theory suggests that there is a large reward from getting the policies "right" since technological growth will lead to more technology. There is most likely no single cause of growth, but rather a variety of factors that lead some countries to grow faster than others.

Hint: Causality

In the discussion of growth, you heard about several factors that are associated with high growth. In the policy debate, it is important to keep in mind that the direction of causality is not always one way.

For example, say that we find that countries with higher levels of education are associated with a greater economic growth rate. One possibility that seems reasonable is that a better-educated workforce will lead to higher growth, and therefore we should follow policies to promote education. Another possibility is that countries with higher incomes and higher growth rates tend to send more people to school because they have more resources to devote to education. In this case, the causality runs in the reverse direction.

Unfortunately it is not easy to determine the direction of causality for many relationships, and both causal directions often sound equally plausible. For example, sound institutions and a stable government seem like they would lead to greater rates of growth. It also seems likely that a strong economy would lead to stable governments and sound institutions.

In addition there may be causality running in both directions. If this is the case, then there is a possibility of a virtuous cycle. For example: more educations leads to greater growth, which leads to more education, and so on. This kind of a cycle could lead to the kinds of growth models that do not have diminishing marginal return and thus behave like the new growth theory models.

Hint: No Magic Bullet for High Growth

It is likely that there is no single thing that a country can do to increase their long-run growth rate – if there was, we would have found it by now. It is probably the case that many of the factors are together necessary to promote growth, but no single policy is sufficient.

The recommendations in this book (and elsewhere) should be thought of as a package of policies to be taken together rather than as a menu from which a country can pick and choose.

PROBLEMS AND EXERCISES

Multiple Choice Questions

1. The convergence result of the Solow growth model states:

    a. Output tends to converge to the steady state
    b. Poor countries tend to grow faster than rich countries
    c. Savings tends to equal investment
    d. Technology spreads across countries

2. The Solow model empirically fails, in part, because:

    a. Technology is not an important part of the Solow Growth model
    b. Some countries have different growth rates than others
    c. Investment does not equal savings
    d. Growth rates have not slowed over time as predicted by the model
    e. All of the above

3. New growth theory focuses on the role of _____ in explaining long-run growth.

    a. Capital
    b. Savings
    c. Depreciation
    d. Technology
    e. Banks

4. Increasing returns to scale in output can explain:

    a. Why growth has not slowed over time
    b. Why richer countries can grow faster than poor countries
    c. Why technology growth may be faster in richer countries
    d. All of the above

5. The idea of learning-by-doing suggests that productivity rises because:

    a. People specialize and thus create increasing returns
    b. The more of a good is produced, the better one becomes at producing it
    c. The work-force is well educated
    d. There is on-the-job training

6. Shumpeter emphasized the role of which of the following in creating a strong and growing economy:

    a. The entrepreneur
    b. Recessions to weed out bad technology
    c. Innovations
    d. All of the above

7. According to the growth accounting formula for the U.S., _____ contributes the most to total output; and _____ contributes the most to per-capita output.

    a. Technology growth; technology growth
    b. Labor growth; technology growth
    c. Capital growth; technology growth
    d. Technology growth; capital growth
    e. None of the above

8. Which of the following can account for differences in growth rates across countries:

    a. Labor quality
    b. Institutional differences
    c. Increasing returns
    d. All of the above

9. Which of the following are implications of new growth theory, but not Solow growth theory:

    a. Countries will grow at different rates
    b. By increasing technology growth, patents will increase the rate of growth of the economy
    c. A change in the savings rate will change the long-run rate of output growth.
    d. Convergence will be true only in countries with similar characteristics.

10. Path-dependency in economics implies that:

    a. Technological change must be analyzed with a view towards its history
    b. Capital accumulation is greater when output is higher
    c. Technological innovation is a smooth process.
    d. Rich countries are better at innovation

True/False/Uncertain

For each of the questions below, answer true, false, or uncertain. Explain your answer in each case.

1. Long-run (40 year average) growth rates have been roughly constant in the U.S. over the past 200 years.

2. The Solow growth model predicts that any two countries will eventually grow at the same rate.

3. Empirically, savings and investment always leads to increased growth.

4. It is impossible to measure technological growth.

5. A patent creates a monopoly; therefore, patents are a bad idea.

6. Technology is produced like most other goods.

Problems

1. Growth accounting. Assume that the production function is given by

    $$Y = A \, L^{0.7} \, K^{0.3}.$$

    Assume that the rate of growth of technology (%ΔY) is 2%, the rate of growth of the population (%ΔL) is 1% and the rate of growth of capital (%ΔK) is 3%.

    a. Find the rate of growth of output.
    b. Find the rate of growth of output per person, %$\Delta(Y/L)$

    Hint: Use the ln trick from above and the production function to find the rate of growth of output as a function of the rates of growth of labor, technology, and capital.

2. According to the growth accounting equation for the U.S. find the rate of growth of technology if real GDP is growing at 2.5%, population is growth at 1%, and the capital stock is growing at 3%.

3. Assume that the production function is of the form $Y = A \, K$. Assume that there is no population growth, and assume technology grows at a rate of g.

    a. Does this function have constant returns to scale?
    b. Does this function have diminishing marginal product?
    c. Find the rate of growth of Y as a function of the rate of growth of K (%ΔK) and %ΔA.

    Assume that savings (and hence investment) is a constant fraction, v, of output, and that depreciation is a constant fraction, d, of the capital stock. Assume that there is no growth in technology. (If you wish, you may assume $v = 0.1$, $d = 0.05$, and $A = 0.8$)

    d. In each period how much does the capital stock increase because of investment?
    e. In each period how much does the capital stock decrease because of depreciation?
    f. What then is the growth rate of K (%ΔK)? Is this positive or negative?
    g. What then is the growth rate of output?
    h. Show this graphically by graphing Y, the savings line, and the depreciation line.
    i. How does this differ from the Solow model?

4. Suppose that the production function is given by

    $$Y = A \, LL^{0.2} \, LH^{0.6} \, K^{0.3}$$

    Where LH is the amount of high skilled workers, an LL is the amount of low skilled workers. Assume no population growth, and that initially half of the population is highly skilled.

    a. How much will Y increase by if LH doubles?
    b. How much will Y increase by if LL doubles?
    c. What would the increase in output be if an additional 2% of the population was trained to become high skilled workers? (Note that 2% of the population is 4% of the unskilled workers.)
    d. Suppose each year, an additional 2% of the total population were trained to become high skilled workers. Would output continue to increase at the same pace? Explain.

    e.   [Difficult] What is the mix of skilled and unskilled labor? That would maximize output? (Hint, note that $L = LL + LH$, and maximize output).

Internet Exercises

1. Data/Graphing. Find the 5 poorest and the 5 richest countries in the OECD, and find their growth rates in the current year. Do the poorer countries tend to have a higher rate of GDP per capita growth than the richer countries?

    See http://www.oecd.org for the data.

2. Go to the U.S. Patent and Trademark Office web site at http://www.uspto.gov/ to answer the following questions:
    a.   What is the process that one must go through to obtain a patent?
    b.   How long does a patent last?
    c.   What is "prior art"?
    d.   How many patents were granted last year?
    e.   How do you copyright (©) something? (See http://lcweb.loc.gov/copyright/).

3. Go to http://www.greatachievements.org/greatachievements/ to see a list of some of the technological achievement of the last century.
    a.   Which of these technologies is likely to increase GDP?
    b.   Do any of these technologies increase the standards of living but have little impact on GDP? Which ones?

CHAPTER 7.
MONEY, INFLATION, AND EXCHANGE RATES IN THE LONG-RUN

OBJECTIVES

1. Define money and describe one of the ways the Federal Reserve Bank affects the money supply.
2. Define the equation of exchange.
3. Use the quantity theory of money to explain the relationship between money growth and inflation.
4. State the long-run dichotomy.
5. Explain how inflation and exchange rates are related.
6. Define purchasing power parity.
7. Explain how economies adjust to private balance of payments surpluses and deficits under fixed exchange rates.

OVERVIEW

The previous chapters examined the behavior of real output in the long-run. The current chapter looks at the flip side by examining the nominal side of the economy, namely the behavior of prices in the long-run. The first part of the chapter focuses on how the level of prices is determined in the long-run by the supply of money according to the equation of exchange. The second part of the chapter focuses on the relationship between currencies of different countries and on the determination of exchange rates in the long-run.

MONEY AND INFLATION

The primary question we are concerned with here is the cause of inflation. To fully understand prices, and hence inflation, we will need to briefly discuss money.

What is Money and Where Does it Come From?

Money is a financial asset that serves three functions. Money is

1. A unit of account,
2. A store of value, and
3. A medium of exchange.

A unit of account means that prices of goods and services are stated in the units of money – in the U.S., the unit is the dollar. The store of value means that money retains its value over time. Finally, money serves as a unit of exchange, which means that it is accepted as a form of payment for transactions.

There are several measures of money, including M1, M2, M3, and L. All of these measures include currency, the amount of checkable deposits and traveler's checks. Each successive definition includes a wider range of assets in decreasing order of liquidity.

The assets included in money come from the financial system. The Federal Reserve can influence the money supply in various ways, but primarily through open market operations – the purchase and sale of government securities.

THE QUANTITY THEORY OF MONEY

As shown in previous chapters, in the long-run an aggregate production function determines output. There is a separate model to determine the price level, which in the long-run depends only on the quantity of money. The separation of the real side of the economy (output) from the nominal side (prices) is called the long-run dichotomy.

The quantity theory of money says that the price level varies in proportion to the quantity of money. The theory is embodied in the equation of exchange:

$$M V = P Y$$

Where M is the money supply, V is the velocity of money, P is the price level, and Y is real income.

This relationship can be converted into a theory of inflation by making three assumptions:

1. V - The velocity of money is constant over time
2. Y - Real output is determined independently of the money supply.
3. M - The money supply is exogenous and causation runs from M to P.

Given these assumptions, the equation of exchange will then provide an equation for the rate of inflation:

$$\%\Delta M + \%\Delta V = \%\Delta P + \%\Delta Y$$

By assumption $\%\Delta V = 0$, and $\%\Delta Y$ is determined by the real side of the economy. Thus an increase in the rate of growth of the quantity of money, $\%\Delta M$, will lead to an equivalent increase in the rate of inflation, $\%\Delta P$. (See the ln trick in chapter 2.)

Empirically, the quantity theory does a fairly good job of explaining long-run inflation rates across countries. However, the relation is not perfect, especially at lower rates of inflation. In addition, velocity has not always been stable and has shifted unpredictably in the past; hence, the quantity theory must be used with care.

!**Warning!** The equation of exchange has nothing to do with exchange rates.

Policy Implications of the Quantity Theory of Money

The quantity theory has an obvious policy conclusion: in the long-run, to control the inflation rate, control the growth of the money supply. Excessive rates of money growth will cause excessive rates of inflation.

The Inflation Tax. It is sometimes possible for the government to pay for goods and services by printing money. Doing this, however, will lead to inflation (via the quantity theory). During inflationary times, the value of the money held by the public will lose some of its value – the same amount of money will purchase fewer goods. This is called an inflation tax.

Seigniorage is the difference between the cost of printing money and the value of the money printed and is thus a source of revenue for the government. Seigniorage can be created by open market operations as wells as by printing currency. The U.S. does not rely significantly on seigniorage as a major source of revenue; however, there have been times and places where it has been more important.

Central Bank Independence. In order to reduce the temptation to raise revenue through the inflation tax and in order for central banks to undertake politically unpopular decisions (such as slowing the economy to fight inflation), central banks have often been made independent of the rest of the government. There is some evidence that greater central bank independence is associated with lower rates of inflation across countries.

THE LONG-RUN DICHOTOMY

The long-run dichotomy states that in the long-run the real sector of the economy and the nominal sector can be analyzed separately. This means that changes in the money supply lead to changes in prices, but have no effect on output in the long-run. This is equivalent to the description of the long-run aggregate supply curve in Chapter 4.

EXCHANGE RATES AND INFLATION

The discussion of prices so far has focused only on the domestic price level. In addition, a change in the price level in one country will affect its economic relationships with other countries.

In order to purchase goods produced in other countries, local currency must be used. Thus in order to purchase a good from abroad, one must first purchase the foreign currency. The "price" of the currency – the rate at which one currency can be change with another – is called the exchange rate. Changes in the exchange rate will affect the cost of domestic goods relative to foreign goods, and so the determination of exchange rates will become important when we begin to talk about export and imports below.

Exchange Rate Determination

The exchange rate is determined by market forces, but may be influenced by government policy. Demand for a local currency comes from people in other countries who would like to import goods and services, or who would like to purchase assets. The supply comes from the reverse, from local people who would like to purchase goods or assets in the foreign country. The intersection of the supply and demand curves will give the equilibrium price of the currency, that is, the exchange rate.

Government can influence the markets by:

1. Choosing whether their currency is convertible - one that people can exchange for other currencies without restriction, or

2. Buying or selling currency in the market to affect its value.

Tip. Exchange rate terminology

If market forces drive a change in the exchange rate we can have two scenarios:

> Depreciation - if the value of a currency goes down relative to another currency.
> Appreciation - if the value of a currency goes up relative to another currency.

If the government, by buying or selling currency in the market then we can have:

> Devaluation - if the government sells its own currency to decrease its value.
> Revaluation - if the government buys its own currency to increase its value.

The Balance of Payments Account

The supply and demand for currency is determined by the amount of demand for goods and assets across countries. The current account tracks the flows of goods and services across borders. The private capital account tracks the flows of currencies across borders when assets are bought and sold. The balance of payments is the sum of the current account and the capital account balances, and must equal zero - since the inflow of dollars must equal the outflow of dollars.

Governments can intervene and, by buying or selling currency, can cause the private balance of payments to differ from zero.

Balance of Payments Forces: Price Levels and Exchange Rates

There is a relation between inflation rates of two countries and their exchange rate. If exchange rates are flexible, then inflation in one country in excess of another will cause depreciation in the first country's currency. Exports and imports will remain unchanged.

If exchange rates are fixed, then the inflation in the one country will cause the private balance of payments to fall into deficit. The imbalance would have to be made up by buying and selling reserves by the government. This situation is not sustainable, as the government will eventually run out of currency reserves and may be forced to allow the exchange rate to become flexible.

Real Exchange Rates

The exchange rate adjusted for price level differences across countries is called the real exchange rate.

The real exchange rate in the U.S. is given by

$$ER = E * (P^{us} / P^{foreign}).$$

When thinking about how the exchange rate changes over time, we can rewrite this as

$$\%\Delta ER = \%\Delta E + \%\Delta P^{us} - \%\Delta P^{foreign}.$$

This equation allows us to relate the exchange rate to the inflation rates in each country. (See the ln trick in Chapter 2 for the derivation.)

Purchasing Power Parity

Purchasing power parity (PPP) theory says that the amount of goods and services that a given amount of currency can buy should be the same in all countries. PPP is based on the law of one price, which states that in competitive markets the same good cannot sell for more that one price. In an international context this implies that PPP will hold, and also that the real exchange rate should equal 1.

This implies that

$$1 = E * P^{US} / P^{foreign}, \text{ and}$$
$$E = P^{foreign} / P^{US}.$$

$$\%\Delta E = \%\Delta P^{foreign} - \%\Delta p^{US}.$$

This also implies that inflation will affect on the nominal exchange rate and not the real exchange rate.

POLICY PERSPECTIVE

Purchasing power parity gives the relation between inflation rates and exchange rates. From the quantity theory, we know an increase in the rate of growth in the money supply will lead to inflation.

When exchange rates are flexible inflation differential across countries will lead to changes in the nominal exchange rate. If exchange rates are fixed, then excess inflation in one country must be met with currency purchases or sale by governments - thus leading to additional prices increases in the other countries - and potentially leading to instability in the exchange rate regime.

In general, the international policy implications of a domestic policy decision must be considered.

CONCLUSION

The past three chapters have focused on the long-run determinants of output and prices. The long-run dichotomy holds that output is determined by capital, labor, and technology as in the Solow growth model, while prices are determined separately by the supply of money and the quantity theory. The following chapters will look at the short-run relationship between output and the level of prices in more detail.

PROBLEMS AND EXERCISES

Multiple Choice Questions

1. Money serves all of the following functions except:

   a. Unit of account
   b. Store of value
   c. Medium of exchange
   d. Value as a commodity

2. Most measures of money include all of the following except:

   a. Currency
   b. Checking account balances
   c. Travelers checks
   d. All of the above

3. The quantity theory of money states that changes in inflation are determined in the long-run by:

   a. The level of unemployment
   b. The level of output relative to potential
   c. The velocity of money
   d. The rate of growth of money

4. Seigniorage is:

   a. A retirement community in south Florida.
   b. The difference between the cost of printing money and the value of money printed.
   c. The amount of revenue raised from an inflation tax
   d. B and C.

5. The Long-run Dichotomy states that:

   a. In the long-run, the rate of inflation equals the rate of money growth.
   b. In the long-run, the real and the nominal sectors of the economy can be analyzed separately
   c. In the long-run, high rates of output will lead to inflation
   d. Output growth is independent of the savings rate

6. The U.S. currently has:

   a. A fixed exchange rate regime
   b. A floating exchange rate regime
   c. A floating exchange rate with occasional government interventions
   d. A nonconvertible currency

7.   The sum of the current account and the private capital account must equal:

    a.   Zero
    b.   Official reserve transactions
    c.   The budget balance
    d.   Foreign savings
    e.   All of the above.

8.   If the U.S. had a fixed interest rate regime, the real interest rate would fall if prices in the U.S. _____, or if prices abroad _____.

    a.   Increased, increased
    b.   Declined, increased
    c.   Increased, declined
    d.   Declined, declined

9.   Purchasing Power Parity theory says that:

    a.   Prices cannot change
    b.   The real exchange rate is equal to 1
    c.   The law of one-price holds across countries
    d.   a and b
    e.   b and c
    f.   All of the above

10. Under flexible exchange rates, a balance of payments deficit will lead to

    a.   A higher price level
    b.   A lower price level
    c.   An appreciation of a country's currency
    d.   A depreciation of a country's currency

True/False/Uncertain

For each of the questions below, answer true, false, or uncertain. Explain your answer in each case.

1.   In the long-run, the rate of inflation equals the rate of money growth.

2.   Broader definitions of money include assets that are progressively less liquid.

3.   The quantity theory of money exactly predicts inflation across countries.

4.   The current account and the capital account can both be in deficit at the same time.

5.   Fixed exchange rates usually require some government intervention in the currency markets.

Problems

1.   What would the current account balance be if the U.S. had $60 billion in capital outflows, $100 billion in capital inflows, and a flexible exchange rate?

2. Suppose that the Fed wishes to maintain a 2% inflation rate in the long-run. Suppose that the rate of growth of Real GDP is 2.5%.

    a. For what rate of money supply growth should the Fed aim?
    b. Now, suppose that, contrary to the assumption of the quantity theory of money, the velocity of money is not constant over time, but it rather fluctuates unpredictably. If the Fed's goal is to maintain inflation at a constant 2% rate in the long-run, what rate of money supply growth should they aim for?
    c. What would happen if the Fed followed a money supply target as in part (a) but velocity was not constant over time, but instead unexpectedly increased?

3. Suppose that money is growing at 6%, real GDP is growing at 2%.

    a. Using the quantity theory of money, what will inflation be in the long-run?
    b. What will be the rate of growth of nominal GDP?
    c. Suppose money supply grew by 2-percentage point to 8%, what will be the effect of this increase on real GDP, nominal GDP and inflation in the long-run?

    Suppose that velocity began, unexpectedly, to change over time, so that it began to rise at a 1% rate.

    d. What could cause such an increase in velocity?
    e. What would happen to your forecasts of inflation if velocity did begin to rise?

4. If purchasing power parity held and the prices in the U.S. doubled, what would happen to the value of the dollar relative to other currencies?

5. Using the equation for real exchange rates,

    a. Find the percentage change in the real exchange rate as a function of domestic and foreign inflation assuming fixed nominal exchange rates.
    b. Find the percentage change in the nominal exchange rate as a function of domestic and foreign inflation assuming that there are flexible nominal exchange rates and that purchasing power parity holds.

    (*Hint:* you can again use the ln trick).

Internet Exercises

1. Go to the bureau of printing and engraving: http://www.bep.treas.gov/.

    a. How much currency is currently in circulation?
    b. What percentage of that is in the $100 denomination?
    c. What does it mean if a given currency is "legal tender" in the U.S.?

2. Data/Graphing. Find the supply of money (M1) and nominal GDP from the 1960 to 2000.

    a. Use these numbers to find velocity in each year.
    b. Generate a graph of velocity over time.
    c. Does this graph suggest anything about how useful the quantity theory of money will be in predicting inflation?
    d. Repeat (a) through (c) for M3.

    See http://www.federalreserve.gov for data on the money supply.

3. Go to http://www.economist.com/markets/Bigmac/Index.cfm and find the most recent "Big Mac index.

    a. In the local currency what is the price of a Big Mac in France? In Australia?
    b. What is the price in these countries when converted to U.S. dollars?
    c. What does "Implied PPP of the dollar" measure?
    d. According to this measure which country has the most overvalued currency?
    e. Why might we expect PPP to fail in the market for Big Macs? Can you think of another good that might be a better test of PPP?

4. Download the following article to answer the questions below:

    Barro: Inflation and Growth:
    http://www.stls.frb.org/docs/publications/review/96/05/9605rb2.pdf

    c. Which country in the data has the greatest about of Central Bank Independence?
    d. Which country in the data has the least about of Central Bank Independence?
    e. What does the author conclude about the importance of Central Bank independence in explaining inflation across countries?

CHAPTER 8.
THE DETERMINATION OF OUTPUT
IN THE SHORT-RUN

OBJECTIVES

1. List the assumptions and implications of the short-run macro model.
2. Show how equilibrium is determined in the multiplier model.
3. Explain how changes in autonomous expenditures and fiscal policy affect output in the multiplier model.
4. Discuss how equilibrium is determined in the money market.
5. Explain how monetary policy affects the money market equilibrium.
6. Discuss how monetary and fiscal policy affects the economy in the short-run.

OVERVIEW

This chapter is devoted to presenting the IS/LM model, which is the basic tool used to analyze short-run output fluctuations. As the IS/LM model is a short-run model we will focus on the aggregate demand side of the economy – in fact, we will see that the AD curve comes from the IS/LM model. The goal of the IS/LM model is to explain how and why output might fluctuate about the natural rate. The keys to understating the IS/LM models are to:

1. Understand individually each of the two primary markets: the goods market and the money market, and
2. Understand how the two markets fit together.

In addition, be sure to keep straight, at each step along the way, which variables are being held constant and which ones are allowed to change. The role of interest rates and investment will be emphasized as an important determinant of output fluctuations.

By the end of the chapter, you should know how to derive the IS and LM curves, understand what causes each curve to shift, and know what determines the shape of the curves. Once you learn the pieces, the IS/LM model will allow you to find the output effects of various kinds of policy.

THE IS/LM MODEL

We begin by assuming a fixed price level. In the AS/AD model this implies that output is determined by the aggregate demand curve. The IS curve is a representation of the goods market as given by the multiplier model. The LM curve is a representation of the money market as given by the supply and demand for money.

THE MULTIPLIER MODEL

The multiplier model shows how equilibrium is determined in the goods market, and how changes in autonomous expenditures affect this equilibrium.

The multiplier model begins by considering aggregate expenditure:

$$AE = C + I + G + (X - M).$$

Consumption is given by the consumption function

$$C = C_0 + mpc(Y - T).$$

Taxes and imports depend on income and are given by

$$T = T_0 + tY, \text{ and}$$
$$M = M_0 + mY.$$

Investment, government expenditures, and exports are taken as being autonomous, that is, independent of the level of income in the economy.

By plugging these equations into the AE equation, we get an expression for the aggregate expenditure. If we assume $t = m = 0$, this gives:

$$AE = C_0 + mpc (Y - T_0) + I_0 + G_0 + (X_0 - M_0).$$

Equilibrium occurs where aggregate expenditures equal aggregate output, or $AE=Y$. Graphically, the equilibrium occurs where the AE line intersects the 45-degree line. Algebraically, given levels for the autonomous levels of expenditure and taxes, as well as the mpc, we can set $AE = Y$ and solve for equilibrium output.

The Multiplier Effect.
The "multiplier" is the amount of the change in equilibrium output when autonomous expenditure changes by $1. In the equation above, the magnitude of the multiplier is $1/(1-mpc)$ and is found by setting output equal to aggregate expenditure:

$$Y = AE = C_0 + mpc (Y - T_0) + I_0 + G_0 + (X_0 - M_0).$$

Solving for Y gives

$$Y = [1/(1-mpc)] [C_0 - mpc(T_0) + I_0 + G_0 + (X_0 - M_0)].$$

A More Realistic Multiplier.
If t and m are not equal to zero, then the multiplier becomes $1/(1 - mpc(1 - t) + m)$. This multiplier is derived in the same way as above

Fiscal Policy and the Multiplier.
Since the government's fiscal policy determines the level of G_0, we can now see the impact a change in government expenditures would have on output. In addition, government spending can play a roll in stabilizing output by working in the opposite direction as any changes in the other autonomous components of aggregate expenditure.

See the tips section below for a useful way to find the magnitude of any change in an autonomous variable.

The IS Curve

The IS curve shows all combinations of real interest rates and incomes where expenditures equal production. The IS curve shows the combinations of interest rates and output where the goods market is in equilibrium.

The transition from the multiplier model to the IS curve comes through investment. Rather than take investment as exogenous, we now specify investment as being determined by real interest rates. The higher the real interest rate, r, (and hence the higher the cost of investing) the lower will be level of investment:

$$I = I_0 - I(r).$$

A change in the interest rate will thus change I, and, through the multiplier model, affect the level of equilibrium output.

$$r \rightarrow I \rightarrow AE \rightarrow Y$$

Since higher r leads to lower I, and hence lower Y, the IS curve slopes downward.

The Shape of the IS Curve. In addition to knowing that the IS curve slopes downwards, reflecting a negative relationship between interest rates and output, it is often important to know the shape of the IS curve, that is, to know by how much output reacts to these changes in interest rates.

There are two components:

$$r \rightarrow I \quad \text{Investment function}$$
$$I \rightarrow Y \quad \text{Multiplier}$$

The greater the sensitivity of investment to interest rates, and the greater the multiplier, the flatter will be the IS curve. The flat IS curve indicates that a small change in interest rates will lead to a large change in output.

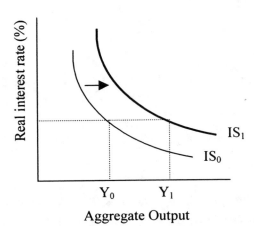

Shifts in the IS Curve. The IS curve is drawn for given levels of autonomous spending and autonomous taxes. If any of these factors change, the IS curve will shift.

The LM Curve

The IS curve is half of the story. With the IS curve we are only able to determine output if we are given the real interest rate. The interest rate will be determined in part by the money market – the supply and demand for money. Once we have this piece – the LM curve – we will then be able to determine the equilibrium level of output.

The Demand for Money

The quantity of money demanded is dependent upon the level of income and interest rate:

$$M^D = M^D(Y, i).$$

Income. Since people hold money primarily to buy goods and services, higher income, which implies more spending, will lead to a greater quantity of money demanded.

Interest Rates. The opportunity cost of holding money is the chance to earn interest. The greater is the amount of money that is held, the fewer interest-bearing assets will be held. So, high interest rates mean that the cost of holding money is high. People will hold less of it, since money plays little or no interest.

This negative relationship between interest rates and the quantity of money demanded gives a downward sloping money demand curve.

Autonomous Influences. In addition to income and interest rates, there are many autonomous factors that determine the quantity of money that people wish to hold. Financial industry innovation (such as ATMs or internet banking) and expected interest rates may both affect money demand.

The Supply of Money

The supply of money is fixed by the Fed, and is represented as a vertical line on the interest rate, money graph at MS.

The Determination of the Interest Rate

The equilibrium interest rate is given by the intersection of the money supply and the money demand curves. By controlling the supply of money, the Fed is thus able to control the interest rate.

The Derivation of the LM Curve

The LM cures show all combinations of income levels and interest rates at which the money market is in equilibrium. To derive the LM curve, we find the effect of changing the level of income on the money market.

When the level of income changes so too will the demand for money. When money demand shifts, there will then be a new equilibrium level of interest rates. The LM curves map out these combinations of income and interest rates.

$$Y \rightarrow M^D \rightarrow r$$

For example, suppose that output were to decrease. This would imply then that fewer transactions are happening in the economy and hence less money is demanded. This is represented by a downward shift in the money demand curve, and hence a lower level of interest rates.

The Shape of the LM Curve

The shape of the LM curve is important if we want to find the magnitude of the effects of changes in output on interest rates. There are two components:

$Y \rightarrow M^D$ money demand sensitivity to changes in income
$M^D \rightarrow r$ interest-sensitivity of money demand

The less is the money demand sensitivity to changes in income, and the greater the interest-sensitivity of money demand, the flatter will be the LM curve. The flat LM curve indicates that a change in output will lead to only a small change in interest rates.

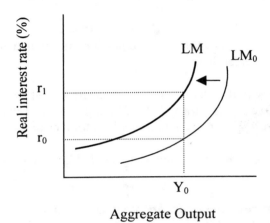

Aggregate Output

Shifts in the LM Curve

The LM curve can shift if, for example, people expect interest rates to change in the future, or if payment technology improves. A change in the money supply will also shift the LM curve.

Monetary Policy and the LM Curve

The Fed controls the money supply. By changing the money supply, the Fed is able to affect the interest rate, and hence the position of the LM curve. Expansionary policy involves increasing the money supply, thus shifting the LM curve to the right.

SHORT-RUN EQUILIBRIUM

Short-run equilibrium for the economy as a whole is achieved when both the goods market and the money market are in equilibrium at the same time. This equilibrium, given by Y^* and r^*, is found at the intersection of the IS and the LM curves.

POLICY PERSPECTIVE: OFFSETTING SHOCKS WITH MONETARY AND FISCAL

The IS/LM model can now explain various reasons why the economy might fluctuate about the natural rate. Economic "shocks" cause there to be shifts in the IS and/or LM curves, thus causing output to fluctuate. Since fiscal policy can shift the IS curve, and monetary policy can shift the LM curve, the government can offset those shocks – such a policy is called aggregate demand management.

CONCLUSION

This chapter has developed the IS/LM model in detail. The next chapter explores further the use of the IS/LM model to analyze policy.

Hint: Algebraic Interpretation of IS/LM

The IS/LM model is presented here in a graphical form. A different way of thinking about the model is to think of the IS/LM model as a system of equations. Each of the "curves" for money demand, money supply, aggregate expenditures, investment, consumption, etc., can be thought of as a separate equation. The equilibrium is then just the solution to the system of equations for the endogenous variables (Y, r, C, I) given the values of the exogenous variables (the autonomous expenditures, money supply) and the various parameters (mpc, m, t).

The IS/LM model is presented graphically to make it easier to see what is really going on within the model.

Hint: How do you know when to shift a curve versus when to move along a curve?

Here is a rule of thumb to use. If there is a change in a variable that is on an axis, then you should move along the curve. If there is a change in a variable that is not on an axis, then you should shift the entire curve.

Example – IS curve.
The IS curve is drawn with real interest rates on the vertical axis and output on the horizontal axis.

- If the real interest rate (on an axis) were to increase, then you would move along the curve to find the decrease in output.
- If the level of government expenditures (not on an axis) were to increase, then you would shift the entire curve to reflect the change.

Example – Money demand.
The money demand curve is drawn with real interest rates on the vertical axis and the quantity of money on the horizontal axis.

- If interest rates (on an axis) were to increase, then you would move along the curve to find the decrease in the quantity of money demanded.
- If the level of aggregate income (not on an axis) were to increase, then you would shift the entire curve to reflect the change.

Tool: The algebra of changes (Δ).

Consider an initial level of some data, X_0. After some change to the system, the value becomes X_1. We can call the change between the initial value and the final value to be the change (D) in X

$$\Delta X = X_1 - X_0.$$

The change operator (Δ) is linear, in that it obeys the same algebraic laws as simple multiplication.

If	$Z = X + Y$,	then	$\Delta Z = \Delta X + \Delta Y$.
If	$Z = a\,X$,	then	$\Delta Z = a\,\Delta X$.
If	$Z = a + X$,	then	$\Delta Z = \Delta X$.

(a is a constant)

In the case of the multiplier, equilibrium Y is given by

$$Y = 1/(1-mpc)[C_0 + I_0 + G_0 + mpc(T_0)].$$

If we want to find a the effect of a change in G_0 on Y (holding all else constant) we can use the rules of the change operator to get

$$\Delta Y = 1/(1-mpc)\,[\Delta G_0]$$

So an increase in G_0 of \$100 will lead to an increase in Y of $1/(1-mpc)$ [\$100].

PROBLEMS AND EXERCISES

Multiple Choice Questions

1. The IS/LM model assumes that _____ is/are fixed and that _____ determines output.

   a. Prices; demand
   b. Investment; supply
   c. Interest rates; supply
   d. Prices; supply

2. The multiplier model assumes that aggregate expenditures are determined by:

   a. Consumption
   b. Investment
   c. Government spending
   d. Net exports
   e. All of the above

3. If taxes an imports are assumed to be autonomous, the multiplier is equal to:

   a. $1/mpc$
   b. $1/C_0$
   c. $1-1/mpc$
   d. $1/(1-mpc)$

4. The IS curve represents equilibrium in the _____ market, while the LM curve represents equilibrium in the _____ market.

   a. money; goods
   b. foreign exchange; money
   c. goods; money
   d. goods; foreign exchange

5. The IS curve is a _____ relation between _____ and output.

   a. Positive; interest rates
   b. Positive; money
   c. Negative; interest rates
   d. Negative; money

6. The IS curve is derived using the multiplier model and allowing which of the following to vary:

   a. Consumption
   b. Investment
   c. Government spending
   d. Net exports
   e. All of the above

7. The IS curve is shifted by changes in:

    a. Autonomous consumption
    b. Autonomous investment
    c. Government spending
    d. Net exports
    e. All of the above

8. The quantity of money demanded depends on all of the following except:

    a. Income
    b. Interest rates
    c. Financial industry innovation
    d. The Fed's decisions

9. The money demand curve will shift if any of the following change, except:

    a. Income
    b. Interest rates
    c. Expected interest rates
    d. Financial industry innovation

10. Money supply is determined by

    a. The treasury department
    b. The Fed
    c. Banks
    d. Consumers
    e. The amount of outstanding currency

True/False/Uncertain

For each of the questions below, answer true, false, or uncertain. Explain your answer in each case.

1. An increase in the money supply will shift the LM curve to the left, causing lower output and lower interest rates.

2. An increase in government spending, holding taxes constant, will lead to lower levels of investment.

3. If investment is sensitive to the interest rate, the IS curve will be steep.

4. If the demand for money is sensitive to changes in income, the LM curve will be flat.

5. Fiscal policy shifts the LM curve while monetary policy shifts the IS curve.

Problems

1. Balanced Budget Multiplier. Consider the standard multiplier model. Assume that

$$C = C_0 + mpc(Y - T_0), \text{ and}$$

$$AE = C + I_0 + G_0 + (X_0 - M_0).$$

To make things concrete, assume the following:

$C_0 = 100,$
$mpc = 0.9,$
$T_0 = 100,$
$G_0 = 100,$
$I_0 = 200,$
$X_0 - M_0 = 0.$

a. Solve for the equilibrium level of output by setting $Y = AE$, and solving for Y.

b. Now assume a fiscal expansion that increases government spending by 100, and sets: $G_0 = 200$. Solve for the new value of equilibrium output. How much has Y increased?

c. What is the value of the government spending multiplier (that is, how much does output increase when G is increased by 1$)?

d. What is the effect on the budget deficit?

Now assume that the government wishes to avoid a deficit, so when they increase G, they also increase taxes, T.

e. Assume now that both G_0 and T_0 increase by 100:

$T_0 = 200,$
$G_0 = 200.$

Solve for the new equilibrium level of output.

f. How much has output increased? What is the government spending multiplier in this case?

g. (Harder) Show that the Balanced Budget Multiplier (the government spending multiplier assuming a balanced budget) is always equal to the number you found in part (g), and independent of the mpc.

2. Now work backwards. Given the economy as in the previous question,

   a. How much would you have to increase spending to increase output by 10% holding taxes constant?

   b. How much would you have to increase spending to increase output by 10% if you wanted to keep the budget balanced?

3. Paradox of thrift. Using the multiplier model, suppose investment is 50, government spending is 130, taxes are 100, and exports equal imports.

   Also assume.

   $$C = C_0 + 0.8 * (Y\text{-}T)$$
   $$C_0 = 100$$

   a. Find the equilibrium level of output.
   b. Find the amount of private savings.
   c. Find the budget deficit.
   d. Verify that investment equals savings.

   Suppose that people become decide to save more money and thus C_0 reduces to 50.

   e. Find the new level of equilibrium output
   f. Find the new amount of private savings.
   g. Explain why this problem is called the "paradox of thrift."
   h. Will this paradox arise in the long-run? Explain.

4. Suppose money demand is given by

   $$M^D = 1000 - 1000\,r + 10\,Y,$$

   where r is the interest rate (in decimal form, so a 10% interest rate implies $r = 0.10$). Money supply is set by the Fed to be 1900. Y is equal to 100.

   a. Graph the money demand and money supply functions.
   b. Find the equilibrium level of interest rates.
   c. Using a graph of the money market, show the effect of an increase in Y on equilibrium interest rates.
   d. Find the equilibrium level of interest rates if Y = 200 and if Y=300.
   e. Use your answers in parts (b) and (d) to graph an LM curve for this economy.

5. Consider again the model from question 1.

   $$C = C_0 + mpc(Y - T_0), \text{ and}$$
   $$AE = C + I + G_0 + (X_0 - M_0).$$
   $$C_0 = 100,$$
   $$mpc = .9,$$
   $$T_0 = 100,$$
   $$G_0 = 100,$$
   $$X_0 - M_0 = 0.$$

This time assume that investment is dependent upon the interest rate as follows:

$I = 200 - 1000\,r,$

where r is the interest rate (in decimal form, so a 10% interest rate implies $r = 0.10$).

    a.   Solve for the equilibrium level of output if $r = 5\%$; if $r=10\%$ and if $r=15\%$

    b.   Use your answer from part (a) to graph an IS curve for this economy.

Internet Exercises

1.   Data/Graphing. Go to http://www.aba.com/Press+Room/ATMfacts2001.htm.

    a.   Approximately how many automatic teller machines (ATM) are there?

    b.   Approximately how many total transactions are there per year?

    c.   Given these numbers, what is the average number of times an ATM machine is used in a day?

    d.   How do you think the increase in ATMs would affect the demand for money?

CHAPTER 9.
POLICY ANALYSIS WITH THE IS/LM MODEL

OBJECTIVES

1. Explain how crowding out limits the effects of fiscal policy on output and how a liquidity trap limits the effects of monetary policy on output.
2. Describe policies that a government must undertake to achieve various interest rate and output targets.
3. Use the IS/LM model to describe three policy actions in U.S. history.
4. Discuss why the interest rate is not always a good measure of monetary policy and why the budget deficit is not always a good measure of fiscal policy.
5. List three implementation problems of monetary and fiscal policy.
6. Explain why policymakers use policy rules to deal with interpretation and implementation problems of policy.

OVERVIEW

Now that you know the basics of the IS/LM model, it is time to learn some of the details of policy analysis with the model. Broadly speaking policy comes in two kinds: monetary and fiscal. These policies can serve two purposes: expansionary policy aims to increase output, while contractionary policy aims to decrease output. It is important to realize that policy actions are usually taken in response to some shock to the economy – so identifying and reacting to these shocks is an important part of policy.

Aside from these broad categorizations, there are a variety of details to consider. This chapter will introduce you to some of the practical problems of policy implementation. Further details are in Chapters 13 and 14.

A CLOSER LOOK AT FISCAL AND MONETARY POLICY

The basics of policy analysis with the IS/LM model are in the following table.

	Contractionary	Expansionary
Fiscal Policy	IS shifts left	IS shifts right
Monetary Policy	LM shifts left	LM shifts right

Fiscal Policy

When the government increases expenditures or decreases taxes, the IS curve will shift to the right. The multiplier model determines the size of the shift to the right.

Note that output does not increase as much as the shift in the IS curve, because the greater level of income means a higher level of money demand and hence higher interest rates. The higher interest rates cause a lower level of investment, and hence output does not increase by as much as the initial shift in the IS curve. This is called the crowding out effect.

In short, the crowding out effect dampens the initial increase in output from the policy change and the multiplier effect. The strength of the effect is determined by the shapes of the IS and LM curves.

Thought experiment: Can investment decline more than offset the increase in government spending?

Expansionary fiscal policy:

> G increase or T decrease
> IS shift right
> Higher Y   output
> Greater money demand
> Higher r
> Lower I (Crowding out)

Monetary Policy

When the Fed increases the supply of money, the LM curve shifts to the right. The money market determines the amount of the shift in the LM curve.

As the interest rate falls due to the increase in the money supply, firms invest more and equilibrium output is increased. As with fiscal policy, the shapes of the IS and LM curves will determine the size of the output increase. A liquidity trap is a situation in which monetary policy has no effect on the interest rate and occurs when the LM curve is very flat.

Expansionary monetary policy:

> MS increase
> LM shift right
> Higher Y
> lower r
> higher I

Achieving Short-Run Policy Goals with Monetary and Fiscal Policy

The effectiveness of any given policy depends upon the shapes of the IS and the LM curves. The shapes depend upon the interest rate sensitivity of money demand and investment demand. (See previous chapter).

If the economy is operating at an output level not equal to potential, either fiscal policy or monetary policy can be used to bring output back. The interest rate consequences, and hence the investment expenditure consequences, are different under each policy, and coordinated policy may be necessary if policymakers have an interest rate goal as well as an output goal.

Accommodative policy is where monetary and fiscal policies reinforce the effects of one another on output, but keep interest rates unchanged. Offsetting policy is where monetary and fiscal policies move in opposite directions to change the interest rate, but keep output unchanged.

REAL WORLD MONETARY AND FISCAL POLICY

Most historical events are more complex than a single shift of either the IS or the LM curve. Real world policy analysis usually involves a shifting of both the IS and the LM curves simultaneously. The effects of fiscal and monetary policy combinations are illustrated with several examples.

PROBLEMS USING IS/LM TO ANALYZE POLICY IN THE REAL WORLD

Since the IS model is a simplifications of reality, as all models are, we must learn how to move between the model and reality. Interpretation problems are problems with knowing how to interpret real-world events within the IS/LM framework. Implementation problems are problems with undertaking the policy.

Interpretation Problems

The interest rate problem.
Interest rates on various assets differ:

1. According to the likelihood that the borrower will repay the loan, and
2. By their term to maturity.

A higher default risk, the possibility that the borrower will default on the loan, will cause lenders to charge a higher interest rate. In addition, bonds of different maturities will have different interest rates because of liquidity differences and differences in expected inflation over the term of the bond. The yield curve shows how interest rates differ by maturity. Typically, longer maturities will have higher interest rates. While the IS/LM model talks about *the* interest rate, it is important to keep in mind that there are really several interest rates in the economy.

Anticipation of policy problems.
The IS/LM model does not explicitly take people's expectations of the future into account. Anticipation of policy must sometimes be considered when analyzing the outcome of a policy change.

Monetary tools and credit condition problems.
The IS/LM model assumes that investment is linked to interest rates. In reality, credit markets are more complex, and interest rates are only one of several factors that influence investment expenditures. Banking and credit conditions are also important determinants of investment.

The interest rate target problem.
Monetary policy in the IS/LM model involves manipulation of the money supply. In reality, central banks announce interest rate targets rather than money supply targets. If central banks target an interest rate (that is, they follow whatever money supply policy that would give an interest rate equal to their target), then instead of an upward sloping LM curve, we have an effective LM curve, which is horizontal at the target rate.

The budget problem: cyclical and structural budgets.
Expansionary policy is usually associated with budget deficits. However, deficits are determined not only by policy, but also by the state of the economy. For example, higher output means more tax receipts. To help separate the fiscal policy stance from deficits caused by economic conditions, we can look at the structural budget surplus or deficit. This is defined to be the fiscal budget balance that would exist when the economy is at potential output. Changes in the structural balance are what are represented by shifts in the IS curve, with an increased deficit causing a rightward shift in the IS curve.

The budget problem: accounting methods.

The U.S. government currently uses a cash flow budget, where revenues and expenses are counted only when cash is received and spent. This can be a problem when the government commits to spending or taxation changes in the future. An alternative is an obligation budget, which includes future obligations in the current budget measures.

Ricardian equivalence is a theory that says that increasing government debt is equivalent to increasing taxes: they both have the same impact of consumption and output. The theory hinges on the idea that people make consumption decisions based on their income earned over their entire life. Since any reduction in taxes that causes a budget deficit must eventually be undone later in order to pay off the deficit in the future. People who take the future into account will tend not to adjust their spending patterns and will simply save the tax to pay for the higher taxes later on. In the extreme, this means that tax changes will have no effect on the IS curve.

Hint. Thinking about Ricardian Equivalence

The best way to think about Ricardian equivalence is to do the following thought experiment. How would you react if the government gave you $100,000 today, but then required you to pay $100,000 in additional taxes tomorrow. Would you spend the money?

Probably not. Instead, you would save all the money and not change your consumption at all.

In addition, the $100,000 in extra private savings would not translate into extra investment because government savings would have decreased by that same amount.

To summarize, because people look ahead in time, they know that any increase in debt must be paid off eventually, so an increase in debt will have the same effect as an immediate tax increase.

There are, of course, several theoretical reasons why this theory may not hold in reality. The evidence suggests that Ricardian equivalence does not fit the data very well. However, the idea that the future expectations of consumers are an integral part of analyzing the effects of a policy action is an important concept in macroeconomics.

Implementation Problems of Monetary and Fiscal Policy

In addition to the problems relating the model to reality, there are also practical problems with implementing the policy.

Uncertainty about potential output.

Since one of the goals of macro policy is to avoid large swings in output, we would like to keep output close to potential. However, we may not always be able to precisely or accurately measure the level potential output. In addition, the level (or rate of growth) of potential output may change over time.

Information lag.

The information lag occurs when there is a delay between a change in the economy and knowing about a change in the economy. While data is gathered fairly often, there is still some lag, as well as some uncertainty, as to what is actually going on in the economy.

Policy implementation lag.
Once we know that a policy is desirable, it then takes time to implement that policy. The implementation lag is a delay between the time policymakers recognize the need for a policy action, and the implementation of that policy. Monetary policy tends to have a shorter lag than does fiscal policy.

How Policymakers Deal with the Interpretation and Implementation Problems

Fiscal policy is rarely used to "fine tune" the economy. Discretionary fiscal policy is usually reserved for major swings in the economy. Automatic stabilizers are programs that are built into the budget to slow expansions and to stimulate the economy during recessions. Unemployment insurance, and a progressive income tax system are two examples of policies that tend to automatically dampen swings in the economy.

THE POWER OF IS/LM

While the IS/LM model has many simplifications and problems, it can still be a very useful tool for policy analysis. The model is also a useful first step towards a fuller understanding of the macroeconomy.

POLICY PERSPECTIVE: UNCERTAINTY AND POLICY IN THE 1990'S

The late 1990's saw GDP growth that was faster than in most of the past 30 years. There were several factors that pointed to different monetary policy options: contractionary fiscal policy and a financial crisis abroad suggested expansionary monetary policy; while high rates of growth suggested inflation might become a problem in the future. Since there were no signs of rising inflation, it could be possible that potential output was growing faster than in the previous two decades.

Uncertainty about the strength of these economic changes and shocks made monetary policy decisions difficult. The Fed reversed policy twice in three years. Despite these difficulties, the economic outcome was judged to be a success.

CONCLUSION

This chapter explored the Policy aspects of the IS/LM model in more detail and presented some real-world problems with using this model. The next chapter will modify the IS/LM model to take into account international trade.

Hint: Automatic stabilizers

The role of automatic stabilizers can be seen in the multiplier model. Let's consider an economy first with no taxes given by $T = T_0 + tY$, where t is a number between 0 and 1.

From the multiplier model:

$$Y = C + I + G + (X - M),$$
$$Y = C_0 + mpc(Y - T_0 - tY) + I_0 + G_0 + (X - M)_0.$$

Solving for Y gives:

$$Y = 1/[1-mpc(1-t)] * [I_0 + G_0 + (X - M)_0 - mpc\, T_0].$$

Lets now consider the multiplier under different values for the tax (assuming mpc = 0.9):

t	$1/[1-mpc(1-t)]$
0	10.00
0.1	5.26
0.2	3.57
0.5	1.82
1.0	1.00

As the tax rate increases, the multiplier decreases. The smaller multiplier means that equilibrium output will fluctuate less in response to changes in autonomous expenditures, and hence the economy will be more stable over time.

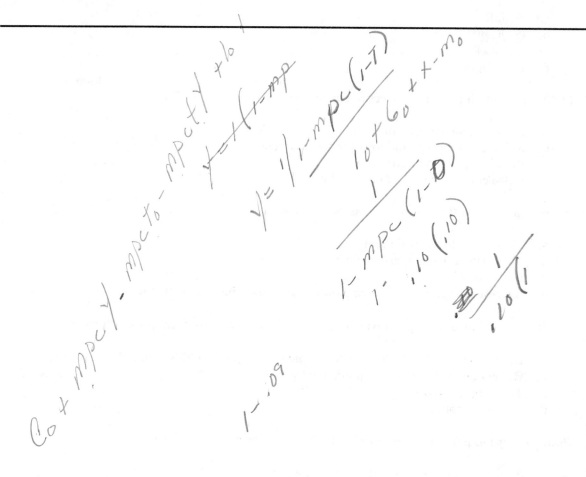

PROBLEMS AND EXERCISES

Multiple Choice Questions

1. Expansionary fiscal policy shifts the _____ curve to the _____.

   a. IS; left
   b. IS; Right
   c. LM; Left
   d. LM; Right

2. Expansionary monetary policy shifts the _____ curve to the _____.

   a. IS; left
   b. IS; Right
   c. LM; Left
   d. LM; Right

3. In the short-run, increases in government spending will tend to:

   a. Raise output and investment
   b. Raise consumption and lower money demand
   c. Raise output and interest rates
   d. Raise consumption and investment

4. Interest rates can differ on various assets because:

   a. They have different default risk
   b. They have different terms to maturity
   c. Both a and b
   d. Interest rates must be the same on various assets because of arbitrage.

5. The budget deficit is not a good way to measure the direction of fiscal policy because

   a. Budget deficits fluctuate with economic conditions in addition to policy decisions
   b. Budget deficits are hard to predict
   c. The debt is too high
   d. All of the above

6. Policy is hard to implement because

   a. There is uncertainty about potential output
   b. There is a delay between when the economy changes and when we observe the change
   c. There is a delay before policy can be implemented
   d. All of the above

7. If policymakers wish to increase output without affecting interest rates, they must follow

    a. an expansionary monetary policy only
    b. an expansionary fiscal policy only
    c. an accommodative policy
    d. an offsetting policy

8. An inverted yield curve shows the interest rate as an _____ function of the _____.

    a. Increasing; money supply
    b. Increasing; bond maturity
    c. Decreasing; money supply
    d. Decreasing; bond maturity

9. If the Fed targets interest rates, the effective LM curve is _____ and fiscal policy has a relatively _____ effect on output.

    a. Horizontal; large
    b. Horizontal; small
    c. Vertical; large
    d. Vertical; small

10. If the Fed pursues a policy that keeps the level of output unchanged; a fiscal policy expansion through a tax decrease (only) will lead to:

    a. Higher interest rates
    b. A budget deficit
    c. Higher consumption
    d. Lower investment
    e. All of the above

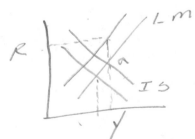

True/False/Uncertain

For each of the questions below, answer true, false, or uncertain. Explain your answer in each case.

1. Since $Y = C + I + G + (X - M)$, an increase in Government Spending by $100 will lead to an increase in output of $100 in the short-run.

2. A decline in the money supply will lead to greater investment.

3. If the economy is experiencing an expansion, the cyclical budget surplus will be greater than the actual budget surplus.

4. Ricardian equivalence says that increasing government debt is equivalent to increasing taxes because they both have the same impact on consumption and investment.

5. The policy implementation lag is thought to be shorter for fiscal policy than for monetary policy.

6. Through the crowding out effect, investment can decline enough so as to more than offset an increase in government spending.

Problems

1. Use the IS/LM model to find the short-run effect of each of the following policies on: output, interest rates, investment, and consumption

    a. A decrease in taxes
    b. An increase in the money supply
    c. A and B together
    d. A decline in exports
    e. A decrease in the savings rate

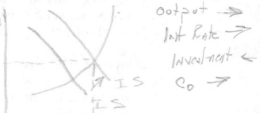

2. Consider again the standard multiplier model. Assume that

    $$C = C_0 + mpc(Y - T_0), \text{ and}$$

    $$AE = C + I + G_0 + (X_0 - M_0).$$

    Because this is now an IS model, assume that investment varies with the interest rate as follows:

    $$I = I_0 - 1000\, r.$$

    Assume the following values for each of the autonomous values:

    $C_0 = 100,$
    $mpc = 0.9,$
    $T_0 = 100,$
    $G_0 = 100,$
    $I_0 = 300,$
    $X_0 - M_0 = 0$

    a. If we assume that the interest rate is 10% (r = 0.1), then what is the equilibrium level of output?
    b. If government spending increases by $100 and the interest rate remains unchanged, how much will output increase by?
    c. Show this shift on an IS/LM diagram.

    From this diagram you should note that the interest rate has now gone up. Suppose that the LM curve is such that the new equilibrium interest rate is equal to 15% (r = 0.15).

    d. What is the new equilibrium output at this point?
    e. What then is the net effect of government spending on output?
    f. In general, what will determine the magnitude of the effect of government spending on output?

3. Suppose that fiscal policy is sometimes used to fight recessions, but never used to slow expansions (since it is politically unpopular to raise taxes or lower expenditures). And suppose that the Fed will pursue policy to both fight recessions and slow expansions. What might you expect to happen to the economy (consumption, investment, interest rates, output, the budget deficit) over the course of many business cycles?

4. Balance budget amendment. Suppose the economy is given by

$C = C_0 + mpc(Y - T)$, and
$AE = C + I_0 + G_0 + (X_0 - M_0)$.

Suppose that taxes are proportional to output:

$T = T_0 + tY$.

a. Solve for equilibrium output as a function of the autonomous spending levels and the parameters: mpc and t.
b. What is the value of the multiplier?
c. Suppose that the $mpc = 0.9$ and $t = 0.2$. How much of an effect on the output would result from a $100 decrease in investment?
d. Why are income taxes sometimes called automatic stabilizers?

Suppose that Congress decides to pass a constitutional amendment that forces Congress to balance the budget every year. In other words, it must be the case that $T = G$ every year.

e. Find the new equilibrium output as a function of the autonomous spending levels and the parameters: mpc and t. (Note: G_0 is no longer autonomous.)
f. What is the value of the multiplier?
g. How much of an effect on the economy result from a $100 decrease in investment?
h. Would a balanced budget help stabilize the economy?

5. Suppose that policymakers would like to increase investment, but would like to keep output at current levels. Describe the combinations of policies required to achieve this goal.

Internet Exercises

1. How long is the delay between when policy is implemented and when it has an effect on the economy? This is an important question for the Fed to answer so they know how much to change policy.

    Check the Federal Reserve's web site to see how long this delay might be.

    See http://www.federalreserve.gov. A good place to look is under Speeches and Testimonies: Humphrey Hawkins testimony.

2. The most recent major change in taxes was embodied in the "Economic Growth and Tax Relief Reconciliation Act of 2001."

    a. How much is the tax plan projected to reduce tax rates?
    b. What was the projected total cost of the plan?
    c. Do you think the tax cut will have a major impact on the macroeconomy?

    You'll have to do some digging here. Start at the Office of Management and Budget (OMB) http://www.whitehouse.gov/omb/ and the Congressional Budget Office (CBO) http://www.cbo.gov/. You will also find a good deal of independent analysis on the topic, as well as a good deal of political rhetoric.

3. It was mentioned in the chapter that anticipation of policy changes may be important. Look at recent economic news and analysis to try to find if people are anticipating any policy change.

    a. Do people expect any major shifts in taxes or government expenditure?
    b. Do people expect monetary policy to change anytime soon?

Start with http://cnnfn.cnn.com. (It will be easier to find reports of monetary policy expectations than fiscal policy expectations).

CHAPTER 10.
SHORT-RUN FLUCTUATIONS IN AN OPEN ECONOMY

OBJECTIVES

1. Explain why the interest rate must rise when income rises to keep the balance of payments in equilibrium.
2. Demonstrate graphically the effects of monetary and fiscal policy when exchange rates are fixed.
3. Demonstrate graphically the effects of monetary and fiscal policy when exchange rates are flexible.
4. Discuss policies other than monetary and fiscal policies that affect the balance of payments.
5. Describe the effectiveness of monetary and fiscal policy for small, internationally open economies using the Mundell-Fleming model.
6. List the advantages and disadvantages of a common currency.

OVERVIEW

This chapter develops the IS/LM model when the economy is open to foreign trade. The analysis and the policy conclusions will depend critically upon whether exchange rates are fixed or allowed to be flexible. It would be helpful to review parts of Chapter 7 before continuing.

THE OPEN-ECONOMY SHORT-RUN MODEL

The balance of payments and exchange rates are additional considerations for government when deciding policy. The private balance of payments (current account balance plus the private capital account balance) is in equilibrium when it equals zero. If the private balance of payments is not equal to zero, the private quantity demand for currency does not equal the private quantity supplied.

An imbalance can be resolved in one of two ways.

1. If the country has a flexible exchange rate, then the rate will adjust so as to bring the private balance of payments back to equilibrium. A deficit implies that the quantity of currency supplied exceeds the private quantity of currency demanded, and hence depreciation will occur to restore equilibrium.

2. If the country has a fixed exchange rate, then the government will have to intervene in the foreign exchange market. A deficit will imply that the country will have to buy the excess supply of its currency.

THE BP CURVE

The IS/LM model is modified to take into account international trade by using a balance of payments curve. This curve represents combinations of interest rate and income levels at a given exchange rate at which the private balance of payments is in equilibrium.

The current account is primarily composed of net exports = exports − imports. Exports are determined by foreign incomes, which are assumed to be exogenous. Imports are positively related to domestic income; hence, the current account is inversely related to income.

> Y increase → current account decrease

The private capital account balance (inflows − outflows of financial capital) is affected by the interest rate. High domestic interest rates (relative to world interest rates) cause an increase in inflows and a decrease in outflows, thus increasing the value of the capital account.

> r increase → private capital account increase

The private balance of payments is the sum of the current account and the private capital account.

Points along the BP curve

The BP curve shows combinations of r and Y such that the private balance of payments is in equilibrium.

If Y were to increase, this would imply a current account decrease. This must be offset by a private capital account increase, which is accomplished by a higher r. The net result is a BP curve that shows that for the private balance of payments to be in equilibrium, higher Y must be associated with higher r.

Points off the BP curve

Points not located on the BP curve indicate that the private balance of payments is not in equilibrium. At points on the left of the BP curve, there is a balance of payments surplus, and vice versa. Again, a surplus implies the quantity of currency demand exceeds quantity supplied.

The slope of the BP curve

The slope of the curve depends upon two things.

1. The responsiveness of capital flows to differences between the domestic and world interest rate. As capital flows become more responsive, the BP curve becomes flatter.

2. The responsiveness of imports to income. The more responsive imports are, the steeper is the BP curve.

Policies that Shift the BP curve

1. Exchange rate policies. Currency depreciation shifts the BP curve to the right.

2. Import controls and export drives. Import restrictions, including tariffs and quotas, will shift the BP curve to the right. Exports drives, including subsidies, will also shift the BP curve to the right.

3. Capital controls. Limits on outflows will shift the BP to the right, while limits to inflows will do the reverse.

Interaction of a Shifting BP Curve with the IS and LM Curves

In general, policies that shift the BP curve will also shift the IS and LM curves. For simplicity, it will be assumed exchange rate policies will be sterilized. In other words, the government at the same time implements policies that offset any changes in the IS and LM curve arising from the exchange rate change.

POLICY ANALYSIS WITH THE IS/LM MODEL AND THE BP CURVE

A government is in internal balance when it achieves its goals for interest rates and output. It is in external balance when it achieves its goals for its exchange rates as well as its trade balance (flexible exchange rates) or its balance of payments (fixed exchange rates). The policy goal is to adjust the IS, LM, and BP curves to achieve both internal and external balance.

Monetary and Fiscal Policy in the Open Economy

Policy analysis in the open economy is conducted with the IS/LM/BP curves simultaneously. As before, monetary policy shifts the LM curve and fiscal policy shifts the IS curve.

If a country has flexible exchange rates, then external balance is achieved through exchange rate changes and a shift of the BP curve. If a country has fixed exchange rates, then policy must be altered to bring the economy into external balance.

Policy That Directly Affects the Balance of Payments Constraint

Exchange rate policy, import controls, export drives, or capital controls can be used to shift the BP curve. Shifting the BP curve allows policymakers to achieve a wider range of internally balanced outcomes while still meeting external balance.

POLICY IN A SMALL OPEN ECONOMY: THE MUNDELL-FLEMING MODEL

An important special case of the open economy model considers a model of a small open economy. The Mundell-Fleming model assumes perfect capital mobility – investors can buy and sell all the assets they want across countries with little cost and risk. In this case, real interest rates are the same across countries. The BP curve, in this case, is horizontal at the world interest rate.

Policy with Fixed Exchange rates

Under fixed exchange rates fiscal policy thus has a large effect on output and monetary policy has no effect.

- Expansionary fiscal policy puts upward pressure on the exchange rate and expansionary monetary policy is necessary to keep exchange rates fixed.

- Expansionary monetary policy must be immediately reversed to prevent exchange rates from falling.

Policy with Flexible Exchange rates

Under flexible exchange rates fiscal policy thus has no effect on output and monetary policy has a large effect.

- Expansionary fiscal policy causes an appreciation of the exchange rate and hence a decline in net exports. The IS curve thus does not in the end shift at all.

- Expansionary monetary policy causes a currency depreciation and hence a shift in the IS curve in addition to the shift in the LM curve.

Monetary Policy and Inflation in the Open Economy

Even though it appears that output in the IS/LM model can be increased indefinitely, this hinges on the assumption of fixed prices. When prices are allowed to be flexible, higher output driven by higher money supply will lead to inflation in the long-run.

Trade Policies

In the case of a small open economy, the BP curve cannot be shifted. Any policy would be immediately offset by strong capital flows.

INTERNATIONAL POLICY COORDINATION

Countries often coordinate policy to achieve macroeconomic goals. There are organizations to coordinate international financial flows, organizations to coordinate international trade flows, and regional and special issue organizations. The chapter examines various examples of international coordination of policy.

Common Currencies

The European Union (EU) is the most prominent example of several countries perusing a common currency.

Advantages:

1. Reduction in exchange rate risk
2. Reduction in transaction costs
3. Economies of scale

Disadvantages:

1. Loss of independent monetary policy
2. Loss of nationalism

There is also a broader question: What is an optimal currency area (a group of countries suitable to adopt a common currency without significantly jeopardizing domestic policy goals)? The technical requirements include: similar industries, significant labor mobility, a broad range of industries, and diverse demand shocks. Political cohesiveness is another requirement for a successful common currency. The evidence that the EU can meet all the requirements for an optimal currency area is mixed.

POLICY PERSPECTIVE

The case of Mexico and several Asian economies in the 1990's illustrate many of the policy challenges facing countries with significant international trade. The choice of exchange rate regime as well as the many components of monetary and fiscal policy represents a complex policy decision. The problem becomes even harder when considering how capital flows can change suddenly.

CONCLUSION

The international flow of goods and services across countries borders introduces another layer of complexity onto the IS/LM model. However, with trade becoming a larger and larger part of virtually all economies in the world, the open economy model is important to understand.

The last few chapters focused on the short-run determination of output, assuming that prices are fixed. The next chapter will allow prices to change in order to form a more complete model of the macroeconomy.

PROBLEMS AND EXERCISES

Multiple Choice Questions

1. In a flexible exchange rate regime, an imbalance in the private balance of payments will be resolved by:

   a. An increase in output
   b. A sale or purchase of currency by the government
   c. A change in the exchange rate
   d. All of the above

2. In a fixed exchange rate regime, an imbalance in the private balance of payments will be resolved by:

   a. An increase in output
   b. A sale or purchase of currency by the government
   c. A change in the exchange rate
   d. All of the above

3. The balance of payment curve:

   a. Shows combinations of interest rates and income levels at which the private balance of payments is in equilibrium
   b. Is a positive relationship between interest rates and income
   c. Will shift when the exchange rate changes
   d. All of the above

4. An increase in domestic income will cause the current account to _____; and an increase in interest rates will cause the private capital account to _____.

   a. Increase; increase
   b. Increase; Decrease
   c. Decrease; increase
   d. Decrease; decrease

5. All of the following will shift the balance of payments curve, except:

   a. Exchange rate polices
   b. Import controls
   c. Interest rate increases
   d. Capital controls

6. Internal balance is achieved when the government achieves its goals for:

   a. Interest rates and investment
   b. Interest rates and the exchange rate
   c. Interest rates and output
   d. Output and trade balance

7. External balance is achieved when the government achieves its goals for:

    a. Exchange rates; and the trade balance or balance of payments
    b. Interest rates and the exchange rate
    c. Interest rates and output
    d. Output and trade balance

8. The Mundell-Fleming model assumes that:

    a. Capital cannot easily be moved across borders
    b. The domestic economy cannot affect world interest rates
    c. Exchange rates are stable
    d. All of the above

9. In the Mundell-Fleming model, fiscal policy is _____ when exchange rates are fixed and _____ when exchange rates are flexible.

    a. Very effective; very effective
    b. Very effective; ineffective
    c. Ineffective; very effective
    d. Ineffective; ineffective

10. In the Mundell-Fleming model, monetary policy is _____ when exchange rates are fixed and _____ when exchange rates are flexible.

    a. Very effective; very effective
    b. Very effective; ineffective
    c. Ineffective; very effective
    d. Ineffective; ineffective

True/False/Uncertain

For each of the questions below, answer true, false, or uncertain. Explain your answer in each case.

1. A private balance of payment deficit when exchange rates are flexible will lead to an appreciation of the exchange rate and an increase in imports.

2. In order to run a trade surplus, the capital account must be in deficit.

3. When capital is perfectly mobile, a country cannot change the domestic interest rate.

4. Since the interest rate is fixed at the world interest rate, the Federal Reserve is powerless in its efforts to change output.

5. A common currency is a good policy when labor is mobile.

Problems

1. Deriving the BP curve. Suppose that imports tend to increase with domestic income and that exports are autonomous:

   $X = X_0$
   $M = M_0 + 0.1\ Y.$

   $X_0 = 100$
   $M_0 = 50$

   a. Explain why imports depend on output, but exports do not.
   b. Find the trade balance assuming $Y = 1,000$, and $Y = 2,000$.
   c. At what level of output will the current account be in balance?
   d. Plot these values on a graph of the current account balance (vertical axis) versus output (horizontal axis).

   Assume that capital outflows are dependent upon the interest rate.

   $Outflows = 150 - 1,000\ r$
   $Inflows = 50 + 1,000\ r$

   e. Explain why outflows decrease increase with higher interest rates, while the opposite is true for inflows.
   f. Find the private capital account balance assuming $r = 0.05$, and $r = 0.15$.
   g. At what level of interest rates will the private capital account be in balance?
   h. Plot these values on a graph of the capital account balance (vertical axis) versus interest rates (horizontal axis)

   Now, we can put these two pieces together to find the BP curve by noting that the capital account balance plus the current account balance is zero. (Assume no government intervention in the market.)

   i. Assuming $Y = 1,000$, what must the capital account balance be equal to?
   j. Given your answer to (i), what must be the interest rate be in order to achieve this balance of payment equilibrium?
   k. Repeat (i) and (j) for $Y = 500$.
   l. Plot these two combinations from (j) and (k) on a graph of interest rates versus output.

2. Open economy multiplier. Suppose that

   $C = C_0 + mpc(Y - T_0)$, and

   $AE = C + I_0 + G_0 + (X_0 - M).$

   Because this is now an open economy model, allow imports to vary with domestic income as follows:

   $M = M_0 + m\ Y.$

Assume the following values for each of the autonomous values:

$C_0 = 100$,
$mpc = 0.9$,
$T_0 = 100$,
$G_0 = 100$,
$I_0 = 300$,
$M_0 = 0$,
$m = 0.2$
$X_0 = 100$,

a. Solve for the equilibrium level of output.
b. Find the effect on equilibrium output of an increase in government spending from 100 to 200.
c. Given your answer in (b), what is the multiplier in this model?
d. Given this result, would you expect opening a country to international trade would help to stabilize the economy?

3. Suppose that a large economy with a floating exchange rate is currently in external and internal balance. On the open economy IS/LM curve, show the effects on output and interest rates of

a. An increase in government spending
b. An increase in the money supply

4. Consider a small open economy with perfect capital mobility. Suppose that there is an increase in the world interest rate.

Find the effects of this change on output assuming no change in policy and:

a. Exchange rates are floating.
b. Exchange rates are fixed.
c. In each case above, what policy should the government follow to prevent output from changing?

Internet Exercises

1. Find the most recent data on

a. Total Exports
b. Total Imports
c. Official transfers
d. Financial inflows
e. Financial outflows
f. Verify that the balance of payments equals the statistical discrepancy.

See http://www.bea.doc.gov/bea/di1.htm for the data.

CHAPTER 11.
AGGREGATE SUPPLY AND AGGREGATE DEMAND

OBJECTIVES

1. State the determinants of the shape of the AD curve and describe what factors shift the curve.
2. State the determinants of the shape of the AS curve and describe what factors shift the curve.
3. Demonstrate how prices and output adjust to shocks to the economy in the short-run and the long-run.
4. Discuss three reasons why equilibrium would deviate from potential.
5. Explain how government can respond to aggregate shocks to the economy and why economists debate how government should respond.
6. Use the AS/AD model to describe what happened to the U.S. economy in the late 1990's.

OVERVIEW

This chapter presents the aggregate supply (AS) and aggregate demand (AD) model of the economy. In the short-run analysis of the IS/LM model, we assumed that prices were fixed. The AS/AD model extends the IS/LM model to take into account prices. The AD curve shows the effect of price changes on output via the IS/LM model. The AS curve will describe how output might deviate from potential. The short-run equilibrium is given by the intersection of the AS and AD curves. In addition, the model can be used to analyze how the economy transitions from the short-run equilibrium to the long-run equilibrium at potential output.

AGGREGATE DEMAND

The aggregate demand (AD) curve shows combinations of price levels and income levels at which both the goods market and the money market are in equilibrium. The AD curve is derived from the IS/LM model of the previous chapters.

!Warning! The AD curve is not like a microeconomic demand curve. In particular, the reason the AD curve is downward sloping is NOT because people demand a smaller quantity of a good when the price is higher. Remember that one "price" in the economy is peoples' wage. So when all prices rise, peoples' purchasing power of their labor does not necessarily decrease.

Rather, the AD curve shows combinations of the price level and output for which the goods markets and the money market are both in equilibrium – in other words, where the IS/LM curves intersect.

The Slope of the AD curve
The AD curve has a negative slope on the price/output graph. The slope is found by examining what happens in the IS/LM model when prices are changing.

The Interest Rate Effect says that as the price level rises, the real money supply decreases, causing interest rates to rise, causing investment expenditures to decline and hence the quantity of aggregate demand to fall. This effect is represented as a shift to the left of the LM curve.

$$P(+) \rightarrow \text{Real M }(-) \rightarrow r(+) \rightarrow I(-) \rightarrow Y(-)$$

Tip. You can think of the price level increase as a decline in the real supply of money (M/P). The price rise has the exact same effect of the Fed decreasing the money supply in the case with fixed prices.

The International Effect says that if nominal exchange rates are fixed, then as the price level rises, net exports will fall; and hence the quantity of aggregate demand will fall as well.

$$P(+) \rightarrow (X-M)(-) \rightarrow Y(-)$$

If the exchange rate is flexible, the exchange rate may adjust to offset the change in the price level. This effect is represented by a shift in the IS curve to the left.

Deriving the AD Curve from the IS/LM Model

The AD curve is derived by allowing the price level to vary, and then mapping out the levels of output given by the IS/LM model. Higher prices, through both the interest rate and the international effects, will lead to lower levels of output.

The larger these two effects, the flatter will be the AD curve – in other words, a small change in prices will have a large effect on output. The size of the interest rate and the international effects are in turn dependent upon the shapes of the IS and LM curves.

Factors that Shift the AD Curve

Anything that causes aggregate expenditure to change (holding the price level constant) will shift the AD curve. Thus any shifts in the IS or LM curve (other than the price level) will then also cause a shift in the AD curve. In particular, since monetary policy shifts the LM curve, and since fiscal policy shifts the IS curve, either kind of policy will shift the AD curve. Expansionary policy will shift the AD curve to the right, and contractionary policy will shift the curve to the left.

AGGREGATE SUPPLY IN THE SHORT-RUN

To complement the AD curve, we will also need an aggregate supply (AS) curve. The AS curve shows how the price level responds to the changes in aggregate demand.

!Warning! The AS curve is not like a microeconomic supply curve. In particular, the reason the AS curve is upward sloping is NOT because firms are willing to supply more of a good at a higher price (since marginal cost increases with quantity). Remember that the price level represents both the costs of inputs as well as the final product, so a higher price level does not by itself give firms an inventive to produce more.

Rather, the AS curve shows how the aggregate price level typically responds to changes in aggregate output.

The Slope of the AS Curve

When prices were assumed to be fixed, we were assuming a horizontal AS curve. With prices allowed to change, we must look to see how output might affect prices. The prices of the factors of production provide one avenue to examine this relationship.

If firms use cost-plus-markup rules, then higher output will lead to a higher price level. Here is the chain that links output to prices:

> Demand for goods and services increases → firms increase their demand for inputs (including labor) → since all firms have greater demand, the market price rises → the firms cost rise → prices increase since there is a markup over costs.

Factors that Shift the AS Curve

Anything the reduces the costs of production independent of demand will shift the AS curve down, and anything that increases the costs of production independent of demand will shift the AS curve up.

These factors include:

- Inflationary expectations – higher expected inflation will lead workers (or other input suppliers) to demand a higher wage and thus force up firm's costs and hence prices. The AS curve will shift up.

- Productivity – greater productivity means more can be produced with less input. And hence the per-unit cost declines. The AS curve will shift down in this case.

- Input prices – sudden increases in the price of important inputs to production, such as energy, will shift the AS curve up.

SHORT-RUN EQUILIBRIUM IN THE AS/AD MODEL

Short-run equilibrium is the intersection of the AS and the AD curves. As either curve shifts, as described above, a new level of output and price will be reached. Shifts in the AD curve cause less of a change in output than in the fixed price case since the price level adjustment partially offsets the initial shift of the AD curve.

LONG-RUN EQUILIBRIUM IN THE AS/AD MODEL

The AS and AD curves describe the short-run equilibrium, but what happens if output does not equal potential? We know in the long-run that output will return to potential (independent of the price level), so we need to describe the mechanism by which output returns.

The Adjustment from Short-Run to Long-Run Equilibrium

The economy is in long-run equilibrium when the AS and the AD curves intersect at potential output. The adjustment process works through the role of expected prices.

If the intersection of the AS/AD curves is at some point other than potential output, then the price level is not what workers initially expected. In response, the workers change their expectations, and hence the AS curve shifts. The AS curve will eventually shift so as to bring the economy back to long-run equilibrium at the potential level of output.

Importance of Government Intervention to Adjustment

The above adjustment will occur without government intervention. However, the government may wish to speed the adjustment (in the case of a recession) or react in some other way to the economic situation. The government's influence on the AD curve must then be considered.

Importance of Expectations to the Time of Adjustment

The speed of the return to long-run equilibrium will depend on the speed and the degree to which expectations adjust, as well as the ability of firms and workers to incorporate these expectations into their economic decisions.

Hint. The AS curve intersects the potential output line at the expected price. The adjustment (if the government does nothing) to the long-run equilibrium takes place by a shifting AS curve.

> AD curve shows how prices affect output: $P \rightarrow Y$
> AS curve shows how output affects prices: $Y \rightarrow P$

WHY WOULD EQUILIBRIUM OUTPUT EVER DEVIATE FROM POTENTIAL?

The adjustment to long-run equilibrium may not take place instantaneously. The short-run equilibrium may differ from the long-term equilibrium for several reasons.

- The Worker Misperceptions Model assumes workers base their decision to work on their real wage, but they may incorrectly estimate their wage because they lack information on prices. Instead they base their decision on their nominal wage. Firms on the other hand are assumed to have full information. Higher AD, and hence higher prices, cause higher nominal wages but lower real wages and hence greater production.

- The Imperfect Information Model assumes that firms and workers lack complete information on absolute and relative prices. Firms confuse a nominal price increase for their good with a real price increase and may produce more.

- The Sticky Wage and Price Models assume that firms have implicit or explicit contracts with their customers that fix prices. Wage contracts, which often last 2-3 years, are the most important example. In this case the fixed prices will slow the adjustment to long-run equilibrium.

In each of these cases, the level of output may deviate temporarily from the long-run equilibrium. However, eventually the economy does return to potential.

AGGREGATE DEMAND MANAGEMENT IN THE AS/AD MODEL

Monetary and fiscal policy can shift the AD curve, and hence influence the level of equilibrium output.

Shifting the AD curve back to its original position with either monetary or fiscal policy can offset aggregate demand shocks.

Reacting to a shift in the AS curve is trickier. How the government chooses to respond depends on its output and inflation goals.

In reality, aggregate demand management is more complicated because of the recognition and implementation lags discussed earlier, as well as uncertainty over the potential level of output, and the effect of their policy.

A Real Business Cycle Perspective on Policy

The AS/AD model presented here is not the only approach to business cycles. An alternative called "real business cycle" analysis focuses on the supply side of the economy and de-emphasize the role of demand. Output fluctuations are determined in this model exclusively by fluctuations in potential output. As a result, output does not deviate from potential, and hence aggregate demand management is of little use.

INFLATION, POTENTIAL OUTPUT, AND THE OUTPUT GAP

The output gap is the difference between actual real output (short-run equilibrium) and potential output (long-run equilibrium). Historically the output gap has varied between plus and minus 6% of GDP in the U.S. over the past 40 years. It also appears that inflation tends to rise when there is a positive gap, that is, when actual GDP is greater than potential.

THE IMPORTANCE OF EXPECTATIONS

The adjustment from the short-run to the long-run in the AS/AD model relies on the adjustment of price expectation. In addition, output may deviate from potential if people make mistakes predicting future inflation. The effectiveness of policy in impacting real output also depends upon expectations of policy.

Reasonable expectations are based on relevant information and past mistakes. This implies that people will tend to not make the same mistakes over and over again.

Rational Expectations are reasonable expectations that are based on the prediction of economists' model of the economy. If we assume that there is a single model that correctly describes an economy, then rational expectations assume that people will figure it out and use it to form their expectations of the future.

Which view of expectations one chooses to use, will imply different things about the effectiveness of policy. According to rational expectations, any expected systematic change in aggregate demand policy has no impact on real output, and only affects the price level.

THE AS/AD MODEL IN AN INFLATIONARY ENVIRONMENT

The AS/AD model was presented as relating price to output. If prices are consistently rising (as they are in most advanced economies), the model can be recast as explaining the relation between inflation and output.

POLICY PERSPECTIVE

The U.S. Economy in the late 1990's provides a useful case study to analyze with the AS/AD model. The conventional view suggests that output was above potential due to an AD shift. An unconventional view suggests that the AD shift also raised potential output. As you can see there are often several different explanations for what might have caused a certain outcome, and hence different predictions and policy recommendations for the future.

CONCLUSION

The AS/AD model extended the IS/LM model to include price determination. Aggregate demand allows policymakers to influence the equilibrium level of output in the short-run and to react to shocks to the macroeconomy. An important part of the analysis is the transition from the short-run to the long-run via price expectations.

At this point, you now have the tools to analyze most of macroeconomic policy. The IS/LM/AS/AD model now explains the level of output, prices, consumption, interest rates, investment, exchange rates, and net exports. We can use the model to find how these factors change when we change any of our exogenous variables including policy variables, such as the money supply or government spending.

The next step is to dive deeper into some of the components of the model, namely consumption and investment, before turning to some details of policy.

Tip: Inflation in the AS/AD model
In this chapter we are explaining how output and the price level are related. The relationship between output and inflation can be derived in a similar matter. So when we say the "price level rises," this can be interpreted as saying that the inflation rate increases. And when the price level falls in the AS/AD model, this is like saying that the rate of inflation decreases (disinflation). The two interpretations are reconciled by noting that in an economy with persistent inflation, the expected price level, as well as the actual price level, is continuously rising. Thus the AS curve is constantly shifting upwards from year to year.

Thought experiment. What must a policymaker know to correctly follow a demand management policy to return output precisely back to the potential level?

PROBLEMS AND EXERCISES

Multiple Choice Questions

1. The aggregate demand curve slopes down, in part, because:

   a. When prices are high, people will demand fewer goods
   b. When prices are high, interest rates will be high, and hence investment will be low
   c. When prices are high, the real exchange rate will be high and net exports will be low
   d. All of the above
   e. B and C only

2. Expansionary fiscal policy causes the AD curve to _____ and the AS curve to _____.

   a. Shift to the right; shift to the right
   b. Shift to the right; shift to the left
   c. Shift to the right; stay the same
   d. Stay the same; shift to the right

3. Expansionary monetary policy causes the AD curve to _____ and the AS curve to _____.

   a. Shift to the right; shift to the right
   b. Shift to the right; shift to the left
   c. Shift to the right; stay the same
   d. Stay the same; shift to the right

4. All of the following will shift the AD curve, except:

   a. Autonomous consumption
   b. Government spending
   c. The money supply
   d. Exports
   e. All of the above will shift the AD curve

5. All of the following will shift the AS curve, except:

   a. Inflationary expectations
   b. Technology
   c. Input prices ✓
   d. Government spending
   e. All of the above will shift the AS curve

6. In the long-run, expansionary policy will lead to:

   a. Higher output
   b. Higher prices
   c. Both a and b.
   d. No change in output or prices

7. The adjustment from the short-run to the long-run is initially caused by adjustments to:

   a. Inflationary expectations
   b. Investment
   c. Money Supply
   d. Consumption

8. Output may deviate from potential output because of:

   a. Sticky wages
   b. Worker misperceptions
   c. Imperfect price information
   d. All of the above

9. Real business cycle theory:

   a. Claims that output can fluctuate around potential output
   b. Focuses on the supply side of the economy to explain output fluctuations
   c. Emphasizes the role of aggregate demand
   d. Assumes that potential output is constant

10. If expectations are rational and prices are free to adjust, aggregate demand policy will have:

   a. A significant impact on output in the short-run and the long-run
   b. A significant impact on output only in the short-run, and in the long-run output will return to potential
   c. No impact on output in the short-run, but a significant impact on output in the long-run.
   d. No impact on output in the short-run, and no impact on output in the long-run

True/False/Uncertain

For each of the questions below, answer true, false, or uncertain. Explain your answer in each case.

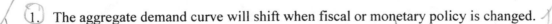

1. The aggregate demand curve will shift when fiscal or monetary policy is changed.

2. Holding the money supply constant, higher prices lead to higher interest rates and lower investment.

3. The aggregate supply curve slopes upwards because firms wish to produce more when the price of their goods is high.

4. In the long-run, the AS curve is horizontal at the expected price.

5. An increase in inflationary expectations will lead to a downward shift of the AD curve, and hence a recession.

6. The best way to react to an adverse supply shock is by decreasing taxes rather than increasing the money supply.

7.   Since monetary policy and fiscal policy both shift the AD curve, the policies will have the same impact on the economy.

Problems

1.   Using the AS/AD model in conjunction with the IS/LM model, show the short-run and long-run effects of the following policy combinations. Assume no foreign trade, and assume that the economy starts at a long-run equilibrium.

     Be sure to show the direction of the impact on output, prices, interest rates, consumption, and investment.

     a.   Tax cut
     b.   Decrease in government spending
     c.   A money supply shift designed to lower interest rates.
     d.   A government spending decrease coupled with a monetary expansion (Early 1990's?)
     e.   A Tax cut coupled with increased government spending and a strongly contractionary monetary policy (early 1980's)

2.   Crowding out. In previous chapters we saw that private investment was crowded out when government spending increased.

     Consider again the standard multiplier model. Assume that

$$C = C_0 + mpc(Y - T_0),$$
$$AE = C + I + G_0 + (X_0 - M_0),$$
$$I = I_0 - 1000 * r.$$

     Assume the following values for each of the autonomous values:

$C_0 = 100,$
$mpc = 0.9,$
$T_0 = 100,$
$G_0 = 100,$
$I_0 = 300,$
$X_0 - M_0 = 0.$

     Assume that the economy was in long-run equilibrium prior to the change in government policy.

     a.   If we assume that the interest rate is 10% ($r = 0.1$), then what is the equilibrium level of output?
     b.   If government spending increases by $100 and the interest rate remains unchanged, how much will output increase by?
     c.   Show this shift on an IS/LM diagram.

     From this diagram you should note that the interest rate has now gone up. Suppose that the LM curve is such that the new equilibrium interest rate is equal to 15% ($r = 0.15$).

     d.   What is the new equilibrium output at this point?

e. What then is the net effect of government spending on output?
f. Show the effect of the new interest rate on an AS/AD diagram in the short-run and the long-run. Assume that the economy was in long-run equilibrium prior to the change in government policy.

From this diagram, you should note that the price level has now increased slightly in the short-run.

g. Show the effect of the price increase on the money supply / money demand graph. What happens to interest rates?
h. Given this result, show the effect of the price increase on the LM curve.

Now examine the long-run outcome of the government spending increase.

i. What happens to the price and output in the long-run?
j. Given all this information, what then must be the new equilibrium interest rate in the long-run? (Hint: What must investment be when output is at its long-run equilibrium?)
k. Given the initial $100 spending increase, how much did investment decline in the long-run?

3. Active Fed. Suppose that the Fed is committed to price stability – that is, they will pursue whatever policy is necessary to prevent prices from changing.

a. Using the AS/AD model, what would be the end result of a tax cut by the government?
b. Show the effect of an adverse supply shock on the economy (say an increase in oil prices).
c. Given the answers above, do you think that this is a good policy for the Fed to follow? Explain.
d. When might this policy work well?

4. Suppose that people set their price expectations according to the simple rule $P^e = P_{t-1}$.

Suppose that the economy starts in long-run equilibrium and that there was then an unexpected shift in the AD curve to the right.

a. Draw the equilibrium before the shift, marking the price level and the expected price level: P^e_0 and P_0.
b. On the AS/AD graph, show the effect of an increase in the AD curve on price and output in the short-run, marking P^e_1 (= P_0) and P_1.
c. At the new short-run equilibrium, are actual prices greater than, equal to, or less than expected prices?
d. In the following year, expected prices adjust and are equal to actual prices in the previous year: $P^e_2 = P_1$. Show the effect of this adjustment on the AS/AD graph and find actual prices P_2.
e. Repeat the process in parts (c) and (d) for another year.
f. In each of the short-run equilibriums, are actual prices greater than, equal to, or less than expected prices?
g. Given the result in (f) are these expectations reasonable?
h. If people had more sophisticated expectations how would the adjustment towards long-run equilibrium look?

5. Which shock? The U.S. economy in the late 1990's was performing very well: output was high relative to the past. At the time there was much debate about what was causing the high levels of output. Consider the following possibilities.

    a. Expansionary fiscal policy with little change in monetary policy.
    b. Contractionary fiscal policy through higher taxes and spending restraint, combined with very expansionary monetary policy.
    c. A one-time shock to aggregate supply arising from a reduction in oil prices.
    d. A permanent increase in the level of potential output.

    Use the AS/AD model to find the effect of each of these policies on output and prices in the short-run and the long-run.

    Assume for the moment that only one of these economic shocks happened. Using the AS/AD model, can we eliminate any of the possibilities if we note that inflation was not increasing during this time?

    If we look back after several years have passed, how would you be able to distinguish between options (c) and (d)?

    Suppose that there was no change in inflation either in the short-run or in the long-run, which combinations of policies from above would be consistent with a permanently higher level of output? Show this combination using the AS/AD model.

Internet Exercises

1. Data/Graphing. Look up data on real GDP and the price of oil over the past 40 years. Generate a graph of the price of oil over time and of real GDP growth over time. Do you see any relation?

    Generate a cross plot of the growth rate of real GDP versus the change in the price of oil in the previous year: i.e. each data point on the graph will be $(\%\Delta Y_t, \Delta P^{oil}_{t-1})$ – see below. How might you explain this finding with an AS/AD model?

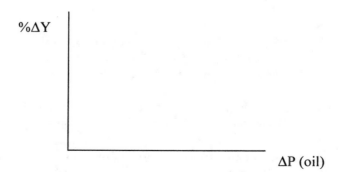

2. Unfortunately, potential output and the natural rate of unemployment cannot be measured directly.

    a. Find an estimate of the rate of growth of potential output. Is the U.S. currently above that rate or below?
    b. Also find an estimate of the natural rate of unemployment (sometimes called the NAIRU: the non-accelerating rate of inflation). Is the U.S. currently above that rate or below?
    c. Given your answers to (a) and (b) what do you expect to happen to the inflation rate?

CHAPTER 12.
MICROFOUNDATIONS OF CONSUMPTION AND INVESTMENT

OBJECTIVES

1. Explain why microfoundations are important for understanding macroeconomic policy.
2. Calculate the present value of a future sum of money.
3. Discuss the permanent income and life cycle hypothesis and describe their implications for macroeconomic policy.
4. Use the concept of the marginal efficiency of investment to describe the relationship between interests rates and investment expenditures.
5. Describe the difference between debt and equity financing.
6. Explain the factors that determine the price of bonds and the price of stocks.
7. Discuss why policy should be viewed as a process.

OVERVIEW

In previous chapters we considered only very simple descriptions of how people decide to consume, and how firms decided to invest. This chapter will dig deeper into the consumption and the investment decisions. Both decisions are inherently intertemporal, that is, they represent decisions over time. Consumers are faced with a decision about how much to spend over time, while firms must weigh the current cost of investment against the future stream of revenue derived from the investment. In addition to learning a couple of tools to analyze intertemporal choice and risk, you will also learn about some of the practical issues involved when dealing with capital markets.

MICROFOUNDATIONS

Approaching macroeconomic relationships from a study of the decisions of rational individuals is called the study of microfoundations. Rather than looking only at empirical regularities, the microfoundation approach starts first from principles and builds up macroeconomic relationships from individual behavior.

The Role of Microfoundations of Consumption and Investment

Microfoundations of consumption and investment depends heavily on intertemporal choices – choices people make over time. Central to this decision process is an understanding of present value – the value today of a future amount.

Present Value

We use interest rates to determine how much an amount of money today will be worth in the future if it is put into a savings account or used to purchase an asset. To determine the present value of some amount in the future, we can just reverse the process.

For an amount of money X next year, the present value is found by using the following equation:

$$PV_1 \ (1+r) = X, \text{ or}$$
$$PV_1 = X \, / \, (1+r).$$

The higher the interest rate, the smaller will be the present value.

For a payment in t years, this becomes

$$PV_1 (1+r)_t = X, \text{ or}$$
$$PV_1 = X / (1+r)_t.$$

The further in the future the payment, the smaller will be the present value.

In general, over many years for a stream of amounts {X1, X2, X3, ... } paid in years {1, 2, 3, ...,} this equation becomes:

$$PV_1 = X_1 / (1+r) + X_2 / (1+r)^2 + X_3 / (1+r)^3 + \dots .$$

This present value idea will be used both when discussing consumption as well as investment.

CONSUMPTION

The consumption function and the marginal propensity to consume (mpc) played an important role in the multiplier model part of the IS/LM model. John Maynard Keynes first introduced the consumption function that we previously used:

$$C = C_0 + mpc \ Y^d$$

Y^d is disposable income (Y-T).

Looking at the data to see if this was reasonable led to an interesting finding.

Looking over long-term averages, the data suggested that C0=0, and that mpc=0.9:

$$C^{LR} = 0.9 \ Y^d$$

Looking at short-term averages, the data suggested that C0<>0, and the mpc was smaller:

$$C^{SR} = 26.5 + 0.75Y^d$$

Put another way, the average propensity to consume ($apc = C/Y^d$) was constant in the long-run, and varied with income in the short-run.

$$LR: apc = C^{LR} / Y^d \qquad = 0.9 \ Y^d / Y^d \qquad = 0.9,$$
$$SR: apc = C^{SR} / Y^d \qquad = (26.5 + 0.75Y^d) / Y^d \ = 26.5 / Y^d + 0.75.$$

The theories presented below were developed in part to explain why we might observe two different consumption functions. Both theories rely on the idea that people wish to smooth their consumption over time.

The Permanent Income Hypothesis

The permanent income hypothesis, first suggested by Milton Friedman, says that people try to keep their consumption expenditures at the same level over their lifetime, and that they decide how much to consume based on their perceptions of their lifetime's average annual income.

Under these assumptions, peoples' consumption in each year of their lives will be equal to the present value of their income divided by the number of years they will consume (n). This value is called their permanent income:

$$Y_p = [Y_0 + Y_1/(1+r) + Y_2/(1+r)^2 + \dots + Y_{n-1}/(1+r)^{n-1}] \, / \, n.$$

This hypothesis can explain the two different consumption functions. If most short-run changes in income are transitory – and thus have a small effect on consumption, since people save much of the transitory income – the mpc will be lower in the short-run than in the long-run.

The Life Cycle Hypothesis

The life-cycle hypothesis, suggested by Franco Modigliani, is a theory of consumption that focuses on lifetime income as well as planned accumulation and decumulation of assets.

The hypothesis says that people save early in life to accumulate assets for retirement. During retirement they dissave and draw down their assets. In addition, people's consumption decision is based on the amount of assets they own.

How Well Does the Life Cycle Hypothesis Fit the Facts?

It seems reasonable to check the theories with the data. In addition to explaining the two consumption function findings, these theories have other predictions.

- Dissaving Among the Elderly. According to the life cycle model, retired people should be consuming their savings at a relatively rapid pace. The evidence suggests that in reality, people do not dissave as much as predicted. Uncertain life spans and the desire to leave an inheritance are two explanations of the empirical failure.
- Consumption Smoothing and Transitory Income Changes. The model predicts that people would like to smooth their consumption over time. However, the data suggests that people do not smooth as much as expected. This might be true if people are not fully rational, or if they are liquidity constrained, that is, they are not able to borrow as much as they would like.

What the Permanent Income Hypothesis and Life Cycle Hypotheses Mean for Policy

The two consumption theories above have important macroeconomic policy implications. These include

1. Permanent versus Temporary Policies: Permanent Policies will have more of an impact on the economy today than will temporary policies.
2. The Wealth Effect and Monetary Policy: Monetary policy can directly affect consumption through its effect on people's wealth via the housing and stock markets (This effect is in addition to monetary policy's effect on investment and equilibrium output.)

INVESTMENT

Previously we assumed that investment was inversely related to the interest rate. We now examine the investment decision in more detail by looking at the investment decisions of firms.

The Marginal Efficiency of Investment

The marginal efficiency of investment (mei) is the rate of return that makes the present value of a project's cash flow equal to its initial cost.

The mei of an investment project costing \$C today and returning a marginal profit X1, X2, X3,… in the future is given by:

$$C = X1 / (1+mei) + X2 / (1+mei)^2 + X3 / (1+mei)^3 + ...$$

The Investment Decision

If the mei is greater that the interest rate, the firm will invest in the project. This is because, the cost of the money required to invest, which is given by the interest rate r, is less than the benefit from investing.

This means that if a firm has many different investment projects, a lower interest rate may lead some unprofitable investment opportunities to become profitable, thus increasing investment.

Tip. Think of the mei as the break-even interest rate. Interest rates lower than the mei mean that the project is profitable, and interest rates that are higher mean that the project is not profitable.

Adjusting for Risk

Firms do not always know the amount of payoff from a particular project, so they must form some measure of the value of a project with unknown payoffs. One approach is to find the expected value of a project.

The expected value of an investment project yielding either $profit_1$ with probability p_1 or $profit_2$ with probability p_2 is given by

$$EV = p_1 (profit_1) + p_2 (profit_2).$$

In addition, if a firm is risk averse, a risk premium is subtracted from the expected value.

Extension: In general expected value of a random number X is given by

$$EV = E[X] = \sum_{x \in \Omega} x \cdot prob(x),$$

where $\Omega = \{x_1, x_2, x_3, …, x_N\}$ is the set of possible realizations of X.

The expected value is like an average, except that when taking an average, all the outcomes have the same probability $(1/N)$.

Choosing a Method of Financing Investment Expenditures

A firm can raise money through several sources including

- Debt finance: borrowing money from a bank or by issuing bonds. Requires fixed interest payments to creditors.
- Equity finance: issuing and selling stock shares. The firm agrees to share profits with shareholders.

Bond Prices and Interest Rates

The price of a bond is determined according to the same principle as the present value calculation. Since a bond is a promise to pay a fixed value in the future, the greatest amount people would be willing to pay for a bond with a payment of X is the present value:

$$P_B = X / (1+r).$$

In general, the PV formula from above can be used to price any bond.

The interest rate to use in this calculation is the interest rate on similar bonds. In addition, the price of a bond will also depend upon the term of the bond and the risk that the firm will default and not pay the interest or the principle. Longer-term bonds tend to have higher interest rates, as do riskier bonds.

Stock Prices

Stock prices can be calculated in a similar way as bonds. According to one theory, the price of a stock will be the present value of the future profits that the share will generate. Risk is an important component of stock prices. A share of a stock that is expected to fluctuate more than average will have a higher return to compensate the owner for bearing the extra risk.

Assessing the value of expected profits, relative to the price of a stock, is thus an important component of current stock prices.

A speculative bubble – inflated prices that are not based on expected profits – occurs when investors buy stocks solely on the belief that they can sell them for a higher price in the future, independent of the present value of the expected profits per share of the firm.

Tobin's-q Theory of Investment

James Tobin's investment theory emphasizes the role of stock market prices in the decision to invest.

$$\text{Tobin's } q = \frac{\text{market value of current capital}}{\text{cost of replacement capital.}}$$

If q is greater than 1 the stock market valuation of the firm's existing capital is greater than the replacement cost – and it is therefore worthwhile for the firm to add more capital by investing.

Tobin's-q theory provides another channel for monetary policy to affect investment. An increase in the money supply will lower interest rates on bonds, and cause more people to purchase stocks, pushing stock prices up. According to Tobin's-q this will then lead to more investment.

Summing Up: Policy Implications of the Microfoundations of Investment

The investment theory leads to some policy implications. Additional policies (other than monetary policy) that affect firm's future profits may stimulate investment by increasing future profits. Monetary policy also has an additional impact on investment via the stock market.

POLICY PERSPECTIVE: THE IMPORTANCE OF EXPECTATIONS

Both consumption and investment theories emphasize individuals and firms forecasts of future events. Expectations thus become very important when analyzing policy. Temporary and permanent policies may have very different effects on the macroeconomy. To assess whether a policy is permanent or temporary, people make judgments as to what government has done in the past – the policy regime. Policymakers' credibility may be important to convince people that a policy that is announced will be enacted.

CONCLUSION

The discussion of microfoundations emphasizes the time dimension of macroeconomic analysis. As such, policy should properly be analyzed not in terms of a one-time policy change, but rather as a sequence of policy actions over time.

The next chapters will dive into some of the details of monetary and fiscal policy.

Tip. Calculating the present value of an infinite stream of income.

A present value of a bond (or other asset) that pays a fixed amount X in every year is given by

$$PV = X/(1+r) + X/(1+r)^2 + X/(1+r)^3 + ...,$$
$$= X/r.$$

Example: If r = 0.1, and X = $100, then PV = $1,000. This is the reason you may see many of your economic textbooks use an interest rate of 10% in many of it's examples—it makes the math just a bit easier.

PROBLEMS AND EXERCISES

Multiple Choice Questions

1. Intertemporal choice represents:

   a. Choices people make about investment
   b. Choices people make over time
   c. Choices people make about consumption
   d. Choices made about what to have for dinner

2. The present value of $110 paid next year with an interest rate of 10% is equal to:

   a. $90
   b. $100
   c. $110
   d. $121

3. Empirically, average propensity to consume in the long-run _____, while in the short-run average propensity to consume _____.

   a. varies with income; is constant
   b. is constant; varies with income
   c. equals the mpc, equals 1
   d. is less than the mpc, is constant

4. The permanent income hypothesis:

   a. Assumes people decide how much to consume based on their lifetime average income
   b. Implies that transitory changes in income have only a small impact on consumption
   c. Implies that permanent changes in income have a relatively large impact on consumption
   d. Explains the empirical consumption puzzle
   e. All of the above

5. The life-cycle hypothesis assumes that people:

   a. Prefer to have a smooth level of consumption
   b. Try to stay out of debt
   c. Consume their annual income
   d. Save money even after they have retired
   e. All of the above

6. The data on consumption suggests that the life-cycle theory may not perfectly fit the facts because:

   a. People tend to react too much to temporary income changes
   b. People tend to react too little to permanent income changes
   c. Elderly people do not consume as much as the model predicts
   d. All of the above

7. The marginal efficiency of investment (mei) is:

    a. The ratio of the profit of a project to its cost
    b. The rate of return that makes the present value of a project equal to its cost.
    c. The present discounted value of an investment project
    d. The nominal interest rate less inflation

8. A firm will invest in a project if the mei is:

    a. Greater than 1
    b. Greater than zero
    c. Greater then the interest rate
    d. Less than 1

9. The expected value of a project that pays $100 with probability 0.2 and $1000 with probability 0.8 is equal to:

    a. 1100
    b. 820
    c. 1000
    d. 800
    e. 120

10. The wealth effect describes:

    a. The effect of increased income on consumption
    b. The effect of interest rates on income
    c. The effect of greater savings rate on output
    d. The effect of interest rates on the stock market

True/False/Uncertain

For each of the questions below, answer true, false, or uncertain. Explain your answer in each case.

1. When bond prices rise, interest rates rise as well.

2. A firm should invest if Tobin's-q is greater than zero.

3. Stock prices are always equal to the present value of future dividends.

4. The wealth effect makes monetary policy less effective at influencing output.

5. Riskier bonds tend to pay higher interest rates, while longer maturity bonds tend to pay a lower interest rate.

Problems

1. Find the present value of an investment project earning $1,000 in each of the next 3 years.

    a. Assuming r = 10%
    b. Assuming r = 5%

2. Suppose that an investment project costs $1,000. The project returns a fixed amount of money every year after the investment is made. How much will it have to return to make it worthwhile to undertake the project if

    a. r = 10%?
    b. r = 5%?

3. Find the mei of the following projects, assuming the cost of each one is $100.

    a. Profits = $110 next year only.
    b. Profits = $100 in each of the next 2 years
    c. Profits = $10 in every year starting next year until the indefinite future.

4. The present value formula the price of a share of a stock this year is:

    $$PV_1 = X_1 / (1+r) + X_2 / (1+r)^2 + X_3 / (1+r)^3 + \ldots .$$

    Where X_t are the dividends paid in year t.

    a. What will be the formula for the present value (PV_2) of the stock next year?
    b. Find a simple equation relating PV_2, PV_1, X_1, and r. (Hint: multiply both sides of the equation above by (1+r)).
    c. Using the result in (b), find the parentage increase in the price of the stock from year to year, $(PV_2 - PV_1)/PV_1$ as a function of the interest rate the dividend rate ($X/PV1$).
    d. Explain in words why the equation in (c) makes sense.

5. Suppose that people consume as predicted by the life-cycle models. Assume you will live 50 more years and work for 20 more years. If we assume an interest rate of zero, approximately how much will consumption and savings change if

    a. A permanent increase in your annual income of $50.
    b. A one-time increase in your income of $1000.
    c. If the interest rate is positive, how might this affect your answers above?

6. Good news? Even good news on the economic front leads to a decline in the stock market. Suppose that it was just announced that GDP grew faster than people were expecting and was above potential.

    a. What might you expect would happen to people expectations of companies' future profits?
    b. How might the Fed react to the news?
    c. In light of the present value equation, how would you expect the stock market to react?
    d. If the economy were below potential, would the stock market react any differently?

Internet Exercises

1. Data/Graphing. Using data from the National Income and Product Accounts, find the annual level of consumption and income since 1960. Graph consumption as a function of Y.

    a. Does this data appear to fit the long-run or the short-run description of consumption as described in the text?

    b. Advanced: Most spreadsheet programs will allow you to generate an equation of a line that best fits the data (usually by least squares estimation). Using the

    For the data see: Bureau of Economic Analysis: http://www.bea.doc.gov/bea/dn1.htm

2. Find a news story that reports on the last time the Fed changed interest rates. What happened to stock prices after the announcement of the move? Was the move expected? Explain the stock market reaction in light of the present value formula.

3. Do some market research on General Electric (Symbol: GE).

    a. What is the price of a share?
    b. How much money did GE make (per share) last quarter? Last year?
    c. What do people expect IMB's earnings per share to be in the future?

    Repeat (a)-(c) for Amazon.com.

    d. For each stock, find the price to earnings ratio (P/E ratio). Why might the two differ?

    (See http://finance.yahoo.com)

CHAPTER 13.
THE NUTS AND BOLTS OF MONETARY POLICY

OBJECTIVES

1. Describe the structure and duties of the Federal Reserve Bank.
2. List three tools of monetary policy and explain how they affect the money supply.
3. Explain how banks create money.
4. Name two operating targets and two intermediate targets the Fed uses to achieve its ultimate targets.
5. Describe the operational conduct of the Fed.
6. Summarize the debate about rules versus discussion.
7. Use the Taylor rule to measure the direction of monetary policy.

OVERVIEW

This chapter is meant to give you a sense of some of the practical issues that are involved in conducting monetary policy. The Fed has a complicated job since by law it is supposed to target maximum employment, stable prices, and moderate long-term interest rates. However, the interpretation of these goals and the way the Fed pursues these goals is open to debate.

THE FEDERAL RESERVE BANK

The Federal Reserve (Fed) is the central bank of the United States. In addition to setting monetary policy, it also performs other financial functions, such as overseeing much of the financial system. Every check you write makes it's way through the Federal Reserve System at some point.

The Federal Reserve System is composed of 12 regional banks. The Federal Open Market Committee (FOMC) is a group of 12 officials within the system who make key decisions about monetary policy such as the money supply and interest rates. The FOMC includes 7 members of the Board of Governors, who are appointed by the U.S. President, and 5 of the district banks' presidents.

The Fed is also a "bank's bank." Commercial banks have deposit accounts with the Fed, and can borrow money from the Fed if they so desire. While formally independent of the rest of the federal government, the president appoints 7 of the FOMC members, and the Fed must report to Congress twice a year on its activities. Its power is derived by law rather than by the constitution, so a law is all that is necessary to revoke its monetary policy authority.

MONETARY POLICY

We described monetary policy as shifting the LM curve (and hence the AD curve.) This process is unfortunately not as simple as drawing a new curve on a piece of paper.

The Tools of Monetary policy

The Fed has three primary tools to influence the money supply.

- Changing the reserve requirement. An increase in the reserve requirement forces banks to hold more of their assets at the Fed or in their vaults. The higher the requirement, the less will be the supply of money in the system.
- Changing the discount rate. The discount rate is the interest rate that the Fed charges banks that borrow reserves. Increasing the discount rate will discourage borrowing and will cause banks to keep higher reserves and thus reduce the money supply.
- Open market operations. This is the tool that the Fed uses the most to influence the money supply. If the Fed sells bonds to the public, they reduce the quantity of bonds in their vaults and replace it with money from the private market – thus decreasing the money supply in circulation.

Open market sale:

The Money Multiplier and Fractional Reserve Banking

The money multiplier tells us the relationship between the monetary base and the money supply.

Money supply = money multiplier X monetary base.

The money multiplier arises because banks loan out a fraction of their reserves and thus "create" money.

The multiplier is related to the reserve ratio (r). The simple money multiplier, which is equal to $1/r$, is the money multiplier assuming no one holds currency and the banks hold no more reserves than what the Fed requires.

$1 deposited into the banking system will yield $1 (1-r) in loans right away. This amount is put into the bank and yields an additional amount of loans equal to $1 (1-r) (1-r), and the cycle is repeated. The infinite sum of these money supply increases is equal to $1/r$.

A more complicated multiplier is necessary if there are excess reserves, or if individuals hold currency. The complex money multiplier shows the effects of these complications. The complex money multiplier is:

Complex money multiplier = $(1+c) / (r+c+e)$,

The symbol c is the cash-deposit ratio, r is the reserve requirement, and e is the excess reserve-deposit ratio.

Since a change in the money supply will lead to a change in the short-term interest rate, we can talk about controlling the interest rate in the same way as we talk about a change in the money supply.

Hint: You may have read in the newspaper that the Fed has lowered (or raised) interest rates. This is just a convenient way to describe what the Fed is doing. When the Fed targets an interest rate, they are really adjusting the money supply as much as is necessary to achieve the interest rate target.

THE OPERATIONAL CONDUCT OF MONETARY POLICY

The FOMC meets eight times a year (about once every six weeks) to make decisions on the direction of monetary policy. The FOMC looks at a variety of economic data and analyses before making their decision on interest rate policy.

- The Beige Book summarizes economic conditions in each Federal Reserve region as is prepared by the regional Fed districts.

- The Green Book provides the members with a two-year economic outlook.

- The Blue Book is prepared by the staff at the Fed and surveys the various economic developments and presents policy options.

(The names of the books come from the color of their covers. Central Bankers are not the most creative people when it comes to naming reports!)

After the meeting, the FOMC votes to determine a direction for policy. The direction is in the form of an interest rate target. Currently the Fed also releases a statement indicating what the Fed sees as being the stronger threat to the economy: inflationary pressures or slow growth.

Operational Targets

In addition to interest rate targets, the Fed has in the past targeted the federal funds rate, borrowed reserves, and non-borrowed reserves. Open market operations are the primary method by which the Fed influences the quantity of reserves. Reserves are also closely related to monetary aggregates, which in turn, have been related to output and the price level.

Intermediate Targets

The Fed has a variety of possible intermediate targets. The money supply and interest rates are the most important. Which intermediate target is used depends on the closeness of the relationship between the intermediate target and the ultimate macroeconomic goals.

Currently interest rates appear to be the better target. However there are still problems. First, there are many interest rates in the economy, and determining which to target is not (yet) an exact science. Second, firms make decisions based on real interest rates, but the Fed can only set nominal interest rates.

Dynamic Monetary Policy and Defensive Actions

Dynamic open market operations are operations undertaken by the Fed to change the federal funds rate. Defensive open market operations are operations to keep the federal funds rate at its current level. Even if there has been no change in policy, the Fed must still buy or sell bonds to keep the interest rate at its current level.

Ultimate Targets

Some have proposed that the Fed should focus on ultimate targets rather than intermediate ones. A zero inflation target, or some specified range for inflation, is often mentioned. (New Zealand went so far as to make it so that the head of the central bank would be fired from his job if there were "inadequate performance" in reaching a target inflation rate.) Zero is thought to be a good target because it is simple and because it would change people's expectations about inflation, thus helping to eliminate it.

The Fed recently appears to look at a very wide variety of data with no single target in mind.

Rules versus Discretion

Rather than make decisions by looking at the data and analysis and making a judgment call, many have suggested letting monetary policy be guided by a formal rule. Milton Friedman suggested a rule that states that the money supply should grow at 3 percent per year. The rule was to have eliminated political pressure on the Fed to expand the economy in election years.

Feedback rules are rules in which the Fed adjusts its operational and intermediate targets on the basis of movements in measures of economic activity that are close to its ultimate goals.

Rules are meant to help solve the time consistency problem—the proposition that people will change their behavior in response to a policy announcement. The problem arises from the fact that the central bank will have an incentive to announce a low money supply policy for the future in order to force down expectations, and then to renege on that announcement later on to boost output. Since people know that the Fed has an incentive to do this, they will not believe the announcement and high inflation will result. A rule (which is committed to) will not have this particular problem (although it may have others.)

The law of diminishing marginal control states that whenever an economic variable is singled out for control, individuals will figure out ways to thwart that control. A rule that initially seems good often becomes less effective over time.

Measuring the Direction of Monetary Policy

The Fed has two primary ultimate goals: low inflation and output near potential (as long as the inflation goal is not hurt.) If the Fed follows a consistent pattern while aiming at these goals we should be able to describe its behavior well. One way to measure the stance of monetary policy is through Taylor's rule.

$$Federal\ funds\ rate\ =\ 2\ +\ current\ inflation$$
$$+\ 0.5\ (actual\ inflation - desired\ inflation)$$
$$+\ 0.5\ (percent\ deviation\ of\ aggregate\ output\ from\ potential)$$

Higher inflation would imply higher interest rates, slowing the economy, and vice versa. We can use this rule to predict what monetary policy is likely to be if we have a specific goal in mind for inflation. In addition, we can use the rule to judge whether monetary policy is currently contractionary or expansionary.

POLICY PERSPECTIVE: FED POLICY IN THE EARLY 2000S

While inflation was still low, the economy was still growing at a rapid pace, in part due to a strong stock market. In a preemptive move to restrict inflationary pressures, the Fed raised interest rates to slow growth. In late 2000 and early 2001, growth did indeed slow. Fearing a recession the Fed significantly reduced rates. In both cases, the stock market appeared to have played a role in the Fed's decisions.

CONCLUSION

The conduct of monetary policy is not an easy job. The potential for macroeconomic stabilization seems great, and most agree that it must be in the policy mix in some form.

The next chapter looks at the complexities of the other major macroeconomic policy tool: namely fiscal policy.

Interpretation: How to set a price

We learned earlier that the price of a bond and the interest rate are inversely related. So, if the Fed wanted to set an interest rate, they could do so by setting the price of bonds. But how do you set the price of a bond that can be freely traded in a market?

More generally, how can someone perfectly determine the price of any asset in a free market?

One option (for the government) is to pass a law that legally mandates a certain price. This solution has the unwanted consequence that a black market may develop.

A better option would be to offer to buy and sell any quantity of the asset at a given price. Buyers would then never accept a price higher than the government's price. Sellers would then never accept a price lower than the government's price. This would then effectively set the price.

By doing this with bonds, the Fed can set the price of bonds, and hence the interest rate. Note that if the Fed wishes to set the price away from the free market equilibrium, then the quantity supplied by the market will not equal the quantity demanded; hence, the Fed will have to either buy or sell some bonds. In other words, the Fed will change the money supply via open market operations!

This interpretation of what the Fed does is just the flip side of the money supply story told above.

PROBLEMS AND EXERCISES

Multiple Choice Questions

1. The Fed's FOMC members consist of all of the following, except:

    a.   Federal Reserve System Governors appointed by the President
    b.   Presidents of the Regional Federal Reserve Banks
    c.   Secretary of the Treasury
    d.   All of the above are included

2. Changes in the money supply will shift:

    a.   The LM and the AD curves
    b.   The IS and the AD curves
    c.   The LM and AS curves
    d.   The IS, LM, and AD curves

3. The money multiplier arises because:

    a.   People consume a fraction of their income
    b.   Banks loan out a fraction of their reserves
    c.   The Fed owns government bonds
    d.   The government taxes are a fraction of income

4. The Fed's intermediate targets include all of the following, except:

    a.   The money supply
    b.   The interest rate
    c.   Zero inflation
    d.   All of the above are intermediate targets

5. The time-consistency problem:

    a.   Says that people should not announce future policy
    b.   Implies that rules are better than discretion
    c.   Is of little importance to policymakers
    d.   Is the proposition that people change their behavior in response to a policy announcement
    e.   All of the above

True/False/Uncertain

For each of the questions below, answer true, false, or uncertain. Explain your answer in each case.

1. The Chairman of the Fed (currently Alan Greenspan) has sole control over interest rates.

2. The Fed can increase the money supply by selling bonds.

3. If banks increase the amount of excess reserves they hold, the money supply will decline.

4. The Fed only engages in open market operations when they wish to change the interest rate.

5. The Taylor rule should not be used because it only looks at inflation.

Problems

1. Suppose that people hold no currency and that banks do not hold excess reserves. Suppose that the required reserve ratio increases from 10% to 20%. Suppose the money base was $1 trillion.

    a. What is the money multiplier for the required reserve ratio of 10%? 20%?
    b. If there were no change in the monetary base, by how much would the money supply change?
    c. Suppose that the Fed did not want to change the money supply. By how much would it have to change the monetary base to prevent the required reserve ratio from having an impact on the money supply?

2. Suppose that due to population growth, the demand for money grows at 1% per year. Given a required reserve ratio of 20%, by how much would the monetary base have to grow to keep interest rates constant?

3. Prior to the start of the new millennium, there was a lot of talk about potential computer problems due to the Y2K bug. As a precaution against mass computer failure, many people decided to hold a greater amount of currency.

    a. If the Fed did nothing, what would have happened to the supply of money as people held a greater fraction of their money in currency?
    b. How do you think banks might have reacted to more people wanting to take cash out of the bank? What effect would this have had on the money supply?
    c. How do you think the Fed should have reacted to this situation if they wanted to keep interest rates unchanged?

4. Assume that the desired rate of inflation is 2%, and it is estimated that the economy operating at potential output.

    a. What is the federal funds target rate implied by the Taylor rule if inflation is 4%.

    Suppose that it is discovered that the estimate of potential was incorrect: we were too optimistic, and the rate of potential is actually 4% below our previous estimate.

    b. If the federal funds rate was initially set as in (a), in which direction should expect the federal funds rate to move in the near future?

Internet Exercises

1. Go to http://federalreserve.gov/policy.htm and find the most recent Beige book report for your region of the country. What does the report indicate about the strength of the economy in that region?

2. Data/Graphing. Answer the following questions about monetary policy.

   a. What is the current target for the federal funds rate?
   b. When was the last time the rate target was changed? By how much was it changed?
   c. What was the actual interest rate on federal funds as of yesterday?
   d. What were interest rates on treasury bonds for each maturity from 3 month to 30 years?
   e. Construct the yield curve. Is it inverted?

Daily interest rates are contained in Release H.15 from http://www.federalreserve.gov/rnd.htm.

CHAPTER 14.
THE NUTS AND BOLTS OF FISCAL POLICY

OBJECTIVES

1. Explain how U.S. federal government spending and fiscal policy have evolved in the U.S. over the past 80 years.
2. Explain how accounting concepts used in the government budget are important for interpreting fiscal policy.
3. State the government budget constraint and explain how each method of financing government expenditures affects the economy.
4. Outline the U.S. federal government budget process and the legislative timetable.
5. List five rhetorical tools politicians use when discussing fiscal policy.
6. Describe the real and financial problems associated with the Social Security System over the next 40 years.

OVERVIEW

This chapter delves deeper into the details of fiscal policy: taxes and government spending. To this end we will look at the government's budget and the constraints on government actions. Since the government, through politicians, determines fiscal policy, we must also consider the relation between politics and fiscal policy.

THE RISE AND FALL OF FISCAL POLICY

The role of the federal Government in the private economy has grown since the 1920's. In the 1950's and early 1960's the use of fiscal policy was accepted as a valuable tool for macroeconomic stabilization policy. Since then the belief that the government could fine-tune the economy through fiscal policy has weakened, and Keynesian style policy has largely given way to a more laissez-fair approach.

The 1980's saw a decrease in tax rates as well as an increase in spending on defense and other programs. The result was an increase in the budget deficit.

> Budget Deficit = Expenditures – Revenues
> Budget Surplus = Revenues – Expenditures = – (Budget Deficit)
> Debt = accumulation of past expenditures – accumulation of past expenditures
>   = accumulation of past deficits.

In an effort to reduce the deficit, Congress passed the Budget Enforcement Act of 1990, which put caps on discretionary spending and instituted a pay-as-you-go requirement, which required new expenditures to be offset by cuts in existing programs, or a tax increase.

Tip: GDP per capita.

It is usually better to think about debt and deficits as a percentage of GDP.

Here's an analogy. Is a $5,000 credit card bill a "big" debt? To you it might be, but to someone like Bill Gates, it's not. The debt to income ratio for you is high, but for Bill Gates it is very low.

So, is a $5 Trillion national debt a large debt? Well, the answer depends on the size of GDP. The debt to GDP ratio is what we really care about, and it better answers the question of how big is the debt or deficit.

What this also means is that it is logically possible to reduce the debt to GDP ratio while still running a deficit.

$$\Delta(Debt / GDP) = \%\Delta debt - \%\Delta GDP.$$

So long as GDP is growing faster than the debt (in percentage terms) the deficit as measured as a percentage of GDP will be falling. This is what happened in the mid 1990's.

Hint. Flow versus stock.

Deficits are a flow, that is, they occur every year, and are usually measured on a per year basis. Debt is a stock, that is, it is an absolute quantity, and will change if the deficit is not zero.

Flow/Stock measures:

- Deficit / Debt
- Savings / Wealth
- Investment / Capital

ACCOUNTING AND BUDGETS

The U.S. government currently uses a cash-flow basis accounting method that counts revenues when they are collected and expenditures when they are spent. The budget calculations do not explicitly distinguish between capital expenditure and current expenditure.

The unified budget includes all expenditures and revenues regardless of their source or destination. The on-budget surplus does not count expenditures and revenues that are designated by law as off-budget items. Social Security is the largest off-budget item, and is designated as off-budget because the surplus are needed to help pay retirement benefits in the future.

Interest Payments and the Primary Budget Balance

Total tax revenue minus all government expenditure except interest payments is called the primary budget balance. The primary budget balance is sometimes used to gauge current spending and taxation decisions without including interest payments, which are the result of past policy decisions.

Real and Nominal Budget Deficits and Surpluses

We really care about the real (inflation adjusted) value of deficits, not their nominal value. The inflation adjustment is done as follows:

Real Surplus = nominal surplus + inflation x *total debt*

When inflation is high, there may be a real surplus even though there is a nominal deficit. This is because the nominal surplus is increasing slower than inflation; hence, the real value of the debt is declining.

Index bonds are bonds whose face value (principle) rises with inflation; hence, they pay a guaranteed real rate of return and have no inflation premium.

THE GOVERNMENT BUDGET CONSTRAINT

The Government faces the same kind of budget constraint as households. Over time, it cannot spend more than they receive in revenues. In any given year total spending must obey the following constraint:

Total spending $\leq$ *taxes* + *newly issued bonds* + *newly printed money,*
G $\leq$ T + ΔB + $\Delta M.$

Taxes

The majority (88%) of total spending is financed with tax revenue. Tax revenue may change because of tax law changes or because of changes in the strength of the economy.

Borrowing

The majority of expenditures that are not financed by taxes are financed by government borrowing. The sale of bonds, called government or treasury securities, is how the government typically borrows money from the public.

The government issues many different kinds of bonds:

Non-marketable securities include non-transferable savings bonds, bonds held in trust funds such as Social Security, and bonds issued to state and local governments. Marketable securities are transferable bonds that the public can buy and sell in the market.

- Treasury bills (T-bills) are sold at a discount and grant the holder one payment at the end of the maturity equal to its face value.

- Treasure notes (T-notes) are sold at face value that pay interest every six months and face value at maturity, which ranges from 2 to 10 years.

- Treasury bonds (T-bonds) are identical to T-notes, except that their maturity ranges from 10 to 30 years.

- Treasury Inflation Protection Securities (TIPS) are bonds that are indexed to the inflation rate, and hence pay a fixed real rate of return.

The Treasury department is in charge of selling these securities through auctions. The debt is purchased by a variety of private and public institutions as well as individuals. The Fed and other U.S. Government agencies hold 45%. Of the remainder, foreign individuals, corporations, and governments are the largest holders.

Printing Money

Generating revenue by printing money, called seigniorage, is currently only a small source of revenue for the U.S., but has been large for some countries in the past. The money is created when the government issues bonds and then sells them to the central bank, which pays for them with money it creates.

Choosing a Method of Finance

The government has the option of financing its spending with taxes or with debt, and there are several reasons why one might be preferred over another.

- Tax Smoothing – constantly adjusting tax rates to finance spending needs may not be practical. Following a tax smoothing policy by letting borrowing fill in the gaps between spending and revenue may be a good idea.

- Reducing the Incentive to Produce – taxes often provides a disincentive to produce. Efficiency and equity are two important considerations when designing a tax system

- Crowding out Investment – public borrowing can compete with private borrowing pushing up interest rates, so a deficit may crowd out private investment.

- Political Considerations – voters usually dislike deficits (in part because they imply higher taxes in the future). However they usually dislike higher taxes as well. This often generates an interesting political balancing act.

ARE DEFICITS BAD AND SURPLUSES GOOD?

Deficits can have negative economic and political effects. Economists like surpluses because they tend to keep interest rates low and thus they encourage investment. Many have argued that surpluses may create a problem, because if the government eventually had to hold assets, it would potentially give the government too much control over private companies.

FORMULATING AND MAKING FISCAL POLICY

The process by which the government alters fiscal policy may have long delays. Automatic stabilizers, which can avoid these delays, are changes in government spending or taxes that result from fluctuations in aggregate income. They require no new legislative action.

The Budget Process

Discretionary spending, which accounts for about 1/3 of spending, is determined through the annual appropriations process. Mandatory spending are expenditures authorized by permanent laws, including spending on entitlement programs such as Social Security and Medicare, as well as interest payments. The process for determining and implementing discretionary spending takes nearly three years.

Changing the Budget Process to Reduce Budget Deficits

In an effort to reduce budget deficits, the budget process has been amended and changed several times. The pay-as-you-go rule, which says that new spending proposals must specify offsets in spending in other programs or a tax increase, is one of the most important of these changes. Other changes have occurred from time to time, changing the ability of government to alter taxes or spending.

THE IMPORTANCE OF FISCAL REGIMES

Since fiscal policy cannot usually be changed quickly, and because politics play such a large roll, fiscal policy is not a great tool for fine-tuning the economy. However, the policy regime – the general rules that determine the direction of policy – may affect expectations of future policy, and hence economic conditions today.

As such, fiscal policy is better viewed as a process rather than as a single policy change.

Spin Control

Since politics plays an important role in fiscal policy, it is useful to examine some of the rhetoric that you are likely to hear in the news. Here are some common tricks:

- Talking about levels, not percentages. Politicians often talk in units of billions or trillions of dollars. Even though the numbers might sound big, they may be small on a percentage basis.

- Front-load spending, back-load taxes. Since budgets are multi-year plans, spending and taxes can be undertaken in different years to make it seem like the budget is balanced, but really pushes the difficult or unpopular policy decisions to future years.

- Take credit for anything good: assign blame for anytime bad. Enough said.

- Use forecasts the make your policies look good. The future is uncertain, as are forecasts, which require human judgment. Choosing the desired forecast from a variety of sources can bolster a policy position.

- Emphasize the positive aspects of data. The economy's data can usually be interpreted in a number of ways. There is always some goods news and some bad news coming out about the economy at any given time.

Tip: In the News

At any given moment, it is possible to find good and bad things about the economy. For example, even in good economic times, millions of people lose their jobs or go bankrupt, and thousands of firms go out of business. In economic booms these numbers will be smaller than in recessions, but there is still bad news. Similarly, even in a recession, there are millions of people who find jobs, or strike it rich.

If the media wishes to do a report on the economy they can always find evidence to support either side of the story.

Government data can give a better view of how the entire economy is doing. But even in this case, there will be a good deal of conflicting data. For example, in early 2001, industrial production was slumping, but consumer spending was strong. We usually don't know for sure what the economy is really doing today until well into the future.

POLICY PERSPECTIVE: SOCIAL SECURITY AND THE LONG-TERM BUDGET PROBLEM

Social Security, which provides funds to retired persons, is one of the largest government programs. It is partially funded, which means that current expenditures come directly out of current revenue—current workers pay the benefits of current retirees.

The Financial Problem

The financial problem is caused by changes in demographics: people are living longer, and having fewer children. When the program began in 1930 there were 30 workers for each retiree, in 2020 there will be less than 2 workers for each retiree. While the U.S. is currently building up a trust fund to pay future benefits, it will not last long – the funds are expected to run out in 2034.

The Real Problem

Another problem arises because there will be fewer workers (as a percent of the total population) in the future, and thus less production per person causing a negative output gap.

Solutions to this problem include

- Reducing retirement benefits,
- Raising taxes on working people in the future,
- Allow immigration to increase the number of workers,
- Luck – hope the productivity grows rapidly

If none of these solutions are undertakes, inflation may be the result.

CONCLUSION

Real-world institutions complicate the implementation of fiscal policy. While in theory fiscal policy should be an important tool to manage the economy, the interplay between politics and policy make it difficult to use.

PROBLEMS AND EXERCISES

Multiple Choice Questions

1. The cash-flow basis accounting method:

    a. Does not include investment expenditures
    b. Counts revenues when they are collected and expenditures when they are spent.
    c. Does not include interest payments
    d. All of the Above

2. The largest off-budget item is:

    a. Social Security
    b. Defense
    c. Foreign Aid
    d. U.S. Postal Service

3. The government budget constraint says that total spending must be less than or equal to the sum of all of the following, except:

    a. Taxes
    b. Newly issues bonds
    c. Newly printed money
    d. Interest payments

4. Discretionary spending accounts for approximately what percentage of the budget?

    a. 25%
    b. 33%
    c. 50%
    d. 88%

5. The Social Security problem is primarily caused by:

    a. Low savings levels
    b. Slow economic growth
    c. The aging of the population
    d. Political pressures

True/False/Uncertain

For each of the questions below, answer true, false, or uncertain. Explain your answer in each case.

1. Deficits are bad.

2. If the primary budget is in balance or in surplus, then the overall budget will be balanced.

3. The real budget debt will always grow when there is a budget deficit.

4. The majority of spending is financed with tax revenue.

5. The budgeting process takes so long that fiscal policy can never be an effective aggregate demand management tool.

Problems

1. Suppose the debt is currently $1 Trillion and the budget deficit is $50 Billion. Find the real budget surplus or deficit if the inflation rate is 10%.

2. From the chapter, we saw that one way to reduce the real deficit is to have some inflation while keeping the deficit low.

   a. Do you think a policy that encourages inflation would work to reduce the real debt? Explain. (Hint: be sure to think about whether or not the inflation is expected, and what affect that might have on interest expenditures).

   b. If it did work, who would lose and who would benefit from such a policy?

3. Suppose that real GDP is growing at 3%, and that there is no inflation. Also suppose that the debt is $1 trillion, and the real interest rate on the debt is 2%.

   a. If the primary budget were balanced, how fast would the real debt be growing?
   b. If the primary budget were balanced, how fast would the debt to GDP ratio (*Debt / Y*) be growing?
   c. What is the largest primary budget deficit that the government could run and still prevent the debt to GDP ratio from growing?

4. It is widely believed that the economic conditions play an important role in presidential politics. A booming economy tends to help the incumbent political party in presidential elections.

   Suppose that the president realizes this and tries to manipulate the economy just prior to an election.

   a. Using the AS/AD model show what would happen to output and prices in the short-run and the long-run if the president tried to increase growth in an election year.

   Now suppose that people become aware that the president will try to manipulate the economy in this way.

   b. Show what would happen to output and prices in the short-run and the long-run if the public anticipated the fiscal policy expansion.

Internet Exercises

1. Data/Graphing. Find the public debt to the penny as of today.

   a. Has it been growing or shrinking over the past week? Year? Decade?
   b. Has the public debt held by the public followed the same pattern? Explain what accounts for the difference between the two.

   http://www.publicdebt.treas.gov/opd/opdpenny.htm
   http://www.publicdebt.treas.gov/opd/opd.htm#history

2. What is the current split of government debt across different kinds of treasury bonds?

   http://www.publicdebt.treas.gov/opd/opds062001.htm

3. What is the status of the appropriation bills in the House and Senate? What is the difference between a budget authorization and appropriations?

   See http://www.house.gov/appropriations/ and http://www.senate.gov/~appropriations/

CHAPTER 15.
THE ART OF MACROECONOMIC POLICY

OBJECTIVES

1. List the long-run and short-run models of the economy and explain their policy recommendations.
2. Discuss how macroeconomic policy to achieve each of the four goals of macroeconomic policy is an art, not a science.
3. Explain how the policy implications of short-run and long-run models can conflict.
4. State the likely causes of 8 macroeconomic problems and recommend a solution for each.
5. Describe the challenge facing U.S. policymakers today.

OVERVIEW

"Given the choice between Bob Solow and an econometric model to make forecasts, I'd choose Bob Solow; but I'd rather have Bob Solow with an econometric model, than Bob Solow without one." - Paul Samuelson

This final chapter summarizes the lessons learned throughout the textbook and draws some additional policy conclusions. Given the complexity of the economy, macroeconomists often operate as much by "feel" as by the rigorous policy models. The quote above shows how human judgment is seen as a necessary part of forecasting and policy analysis.

FOUR BROAD POLICY LESSONS

The book emphasized four broad policy lessons:

1. Models do not provide direct policy answers.
2. Macroeconomic policy inevitably involves tradeoffs.
3. Growth requires getting institutions and incentives right.
4. Monetary and fiscal policy can help stabilize the economy.

A REVIEW

The books was divided in to five sections:

1. Introduction to intermediate macroeconomics. This was an introduction to the basic concepts, data, and goals.

2. The foundations long-run macroeconomic policy. On the real side of the economy, long-run growth analysis was conducted with the Solow growth model, and its weaknesses were examined. On the nominal side, the quantity theory was used to analyze prices.

3. The foundations of short-run macroeconomic policy. The IS/LM model and the multiplier model were the core of the short-run analysis. The model was also extended to the open economy. The AS/AD model then extended the IS/LM model to allow for flexible prices. Finally, the microfoundations of consumption and investment were investigated to show how policy analysis must take into account aspects of intertemporal choice.

4. The nuts and bolts of macroeconomic policy. This section looks at the practical problems that are involved when analyzing monetary and fiscal policy.

5. The art of macroeconomic policy. This sections provides a review of the material with the four broad policy lessons in mind.

The Conflicts between the Long-run and the Short-run

The policy recommendations that are suggested by the long-run and short-run models occasionally conflict. Macroeconomics would be a lot easier (and less interesting!) if we had a single model with simple conclusions. However, since the economy is a very complicated system, we shouldn't be surprised that we haven't discovered a single unifying model.

THE GOALS OF POLICY

Early in the book, we mentioned several goals of policymakers. This chapter reviews some of the policy recommendations for each of these goals. For each goal, the policy recommendation is a combination of analysis using the models developed in the textbook and a view of the weaknesses and simplifications of the models. Looking at past economic conditions and policies are often helpful in developing an intuition, or a "feel," for how the economy works.

The goals:

- High Growth
- Low Inflation
- Low Unemployment
- Smooth growth in output

Conventional Wisdom

While economists often disagree about a variety of economic policies, there is also a core of agreement. The text lists several of these areas.

POLICY FOR THE NEW ECONOMY

The U.S. economy between the end of the recession in the early 1900s and through the beginning of the new millennium performed very well, even better than most had predicted. Whether this was caused by good policies, favorable supply shocks, global competition, greater technology growth, or pure luck is open to debate. Most likely it was a combinations of factors.

Many took the view that the economy had fundamentally changed, and hence policy should be adjusted accordingly. On the other side, some argued that since it is costly to reduce inflation once it has accelerated, we should be cautions.

CONCLUSION

The models and analysis in this book were meant to teach you tools and a style of analysis rather than specific policy prescriptions (although we did see many of those as well.) It is the combination of formal analysis and common sense that make a good economist and good economic policy.

ANSWERS TO PROBLEMS

CHAPTER 1

Multiple Choice

1. e. A high value for the domestic currency is not necessarily desirable by itself. An appreciation may be used for other purposes consistent with other international goals.

2. d. The other choices are demand management policies.

3. b. This is approximately the real growth rate of GDP in the U.S.

4. c. Expansions are the norm, while recessions are shorter.

5. d. A model can be presented in many ways – not necessarily algebraically.

True/False/Uncertain

1. False. The economy will tend to move back to the natural rate over time; but the policymakers may want lower unemployment if possible.

2. False. Inflation implies that the CPI is rising. The CPI is an *average* of all prices, so while some prices are rising, it is possible for others to be falling.

3. False. The budget balance is determined by taxes and expenditures; however, these amounts will vary with economic conditions as well as policy decisions.

4. True. This is just about the definition of a model.

5. False. When output is *above* potential, inflation tends to rise.

Chapter 2

Multiple Choice

1. d. GDP includes all final production, not just production consumed by firms.

2. c. Since the Deflator = Nominal GDP / Real GDP. It is also likely that the CPI will be falling as well, but we can't tell this for sure with on the GDP numbers

3. b. The other three options characterize both the CPI and the deflator. The CPI is based on what consumers buy, so it includes imports, but not exports. The deflator, on the other hand, includes all production – including goods and services that firms tend to purchase as well as those goods primarily purchased by the government and exports. The weight placed on each good in the basket is different as well.

4. e. All of the above. The total bias is thought to be around 1%. So measured inflation is about 1% higher that a measure which takes these biases into account.

5. d. Discouraged workers and retired people are not in the labor force. Employed people are part of the employed group even if they are looking for jobs.

6. a. About 2/3 of GDP is consumption expenditure.

7. a. Employee compensation is about 71% of total national income.

8. c. The PPI is the Producer Price Index. It measures goods and services purchased by producers in roughly the same way as the CPI measures prices for consumers.

9. b. A peak is when the recession starts. A trough is when it ends.

10. a. Net Exports = Trade Surplus = Exports – Imports.

True/False/Uncertain

1. True. GDP measures production on domestic soil. The plant's sales would not be included in GNP, however.

2. False. A complete business cycle is usually defined as peak-peak or trough-trough. A *recession* begins at a peak and ends in a trough.

3. False. The trade deficit has been increasing; which is the same as saying that the trade surplus has been *decreasing*. In addition, the change has not been very steady, but has fluctuated from year to year.

4. False, but almost true. Occasionally there are interventions by the government, but they have been relatively rare.

5. False. There are many people who no not want jobs, including retired people, students, etc, who are not in the labor force.

Problems

1. Calculating GDP.

   a. Nominal GDP in 2000 is 10 * \$1 + 10 * \$2 = \$30;
      Nominal GDP in 2001 is 12 * \$1 + 15 * \$2.20 = \$45.

   b. The growth rate is then (45 − 30) / 30 = 15/30 = 0.5 or 50%.

   c. Real GDP, using 2000 as the base year is:
      Real GDP 2000: \$30
      Real GDP 2001: 12 * \$1 + 15 * \$2 = \$42

   d. Real GDP growth is 42 − 30 / 30 = 12/30 = 0.4 or 40%

   e. Deflator = Nominal GDP / Real GDP X 100 =
      In 2000 Deflator = 30/30 X 100 = 100
      In 2001 Deflator = 45 / 42 X 100 = 107.1

   f. Inflation = (107.1 − 100) / 100 = 0.071 or 7.1%

2. GDP.

   a. Fisherman: 30\$ of value added.
      Canning company: (100*1\$) - (30\$+0.1*100) - \$30 = \$100 − \$40 = \$60.
      Restaurant: 200*\$3 − (100*\$1 + 10*\$1) = \$490

      Total value added = 30 + 60 + 490 = \$580.

   b. The final value of goods and service is the sales by the restaurant to the final consumer and are equal to 200*3\$ = \$600.

   c. The reason these two measures are not equal is that in part (a) there were two additional firms—the can manufacturer and the bread maker—that were not included in the valued added calculation. If these two firms were included then the two measures would be equal.

3. Inflation adjustment:

   a. The price increase was $\%\Delta P$ = (172.2 - 82.4) / 82.4 = 89.8 / 82.4 = 1.09 or 109%

   b. The annual rate of inflation over these 20 years is then $(1+\%\Delta P^a)^{20}$ = (1+1.09). This then gives $\%\Delta P^a = (1+1.09)^{1/20} − 1$. And $\%\Delta P$ = 3.75%.

   c. Car increased by: (22,000- 5,400) / 5,400 = 3.07 or 307%

   d. The 5,400 \$(1980) car would cost: 5,400 \$(1980) * 172.2 / 82.4 = 11,285 \$(2000). Another way to calculate this would be 5,400 (1 + $\%\Delta P$) = 5,400 * 2.09 = 11,285 \$(2000).

e. The 22,000 $(1980) car would cost: 22,000 $(2000) * 82.4 / 172.2 = 10,527 $(1980). Another way to calculate this would be 22,000 / (1 + %ΔP) = 22,000 / 2.09 = 10,527 $(1980).

f. The price of a care *relative* to other goods and services in the economy has risen over this time period.

g. This might be a misleading statement for at least three reasons. First, the quality of cars is probably much higher today than in 1980. Second, the average price of a car might be misleading—suppose that people are buying more SUV's and fewer budget cars in 2000. The average price might reflect a change in the mix of car being purchased rather than a change in the price of any given car. Finally, people's real incomes have on average increased as well, so the percentage of someone's income required to purchase a car has not necessarily increased.

4. Labor market.

a. The unemployment rate is 5,994 / 141,858 = 4.2%

b. The employment rate is 135,864 / 141,858 = 95.8%

c. The labor force participation rate is (labor force / population) = (141,858) / (69,171 + 141,858) = 67%

5. Growth rates.

Note that since

GDP deflator = nominal GDP / real GDP

we can use the ln trick as follows:

ln (GDP deflator) = ln (nominal GDP) – ln (real GDP);

which implies that

%Δ (GDP deflator) = %Δ (nominal GDP) – %Δ (real GDP), and

Growth rate of GDP deflator = Growth rate of nominal GDP – Growth rate of real GDP);

a. From the above equation, note that:
Real GDP growth = Nominal GDP growth – GDP deflator growth.

And hence Real GDP growth = 6.5% - 3% = 3.5%

b. Using the same trick, %Δ(Y/L) = %ΔY – %ΔL. = 3.5% - 1% = 2.5%.

c. %Δ(W/P) = %ΔW – %ΔP = 5.5% – 3% = 2.5%

CHAPTER 3

Multiple Choice

1. d. Even though prices are higher, so to are people's nominal wages, so inflation does not by itself lead to less real purchasing power.

2. d. An unexpected decline in inflation will lead to real interest rates that are higher than expected, benefiting lenders.

3. c. The lower the cost of matching, the faster people will find jobs and hence the greater will be the flows out of the unemployment pool. This will lead to a lower natural rate of unemployment.

4. c. All of the other factors will lead to a change in the natural rate, not cyclical unemployment.

5. b. Okun's law is $\%\Delta Q = 3.5 - (2 \cdot \Delta U)$.

6. c. The Phillips curve is an empirical relationship between inflation and unemployment

7. c. The sacrifice ratio gives the cost of reducing inflation as measured by the percent of output reduction necessary to reduce inflation by 1 percentage point.

8. b. Flows in both directions between employment and not in the labor force total 6.5 million per month.

9. e. There appears to be no single factor causing the shift. All have probably played some role, although demographics (aging baby boomers) and the growth in temp agencies appear to have had the largest effects.

10. a. Insider-outsider unemployment arises when insiders can push up their wages.

True/False/Uncertain

1. False. The average spell is about 3 weeks. The median is about 5 weeks.

2. False. Extremely low unemployment may make it very hard for firms to hire workers; and so some unemployment may be beneficial.

3. False. The *long-run AS* curve is vertical. This is true because in the long-run output returns to potential output.

4. False. In the long-run, lower inflation is thought to be good for the economy, except perhaps at very low levels. If nominal wages are unable to freely adjust, then some inflation can provide some grease to the labor market to allow real wages to decline.

5. False. Women tend to have only slightly higher unemployment rates. Teenagers, African Americans, and people of Hispanic origin tend to have higher unemployment rates as well.

Problems

1. Labor market.

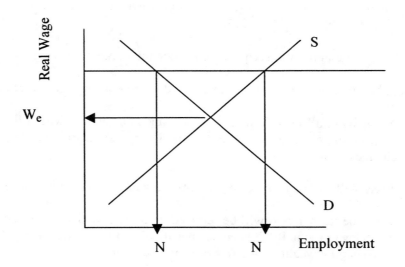

If the real wage is above the equilibrium wage, W_e, there will be unemployment. Unemployment is given by $N_1 - N_2$.

2. Matched Supply and Demand.

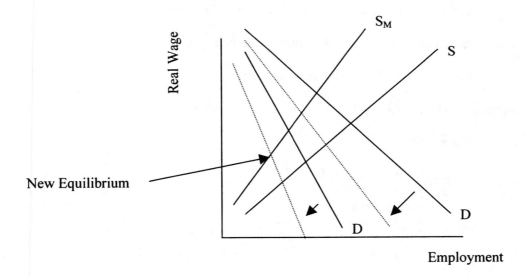

   a. Employment declines.
   b. Frictional rate of unemployment declines slightly.
   c. Wages decline.

This shift might be caused by an economic downturn.

3. If inflation was at 4%, this means, according to the Phillips curve, that unemployment was at (10-4) / 2 = 3%.

Moving from 4% inflation to 3% would require unemployment increasing to (10-3)/2 = 3.5%.

This 0.5 percentage point increase in unemployment (ΔU) would cost, via Okun's rule, that output was reduced from 3.5% to 2.5%.

So, the 1% decline in inflation required a 1% decline in output; giving a sacrifice ratio of 1.

4. Deflation. Many of the same costs of inflation do not go away when prices are falling.

    a. There will still be information costs, since consumers will still have to try to infer the relative price of goods, and try to distinguish between relative and absolute price changes.

    b. There will still be menu costs as firms now must lower their prices rather than raise them.

    c. The shoe leather cost will be reduced. If there is deflation, the cost of holding money is much lower (actually, it becomes negative!). In this case, there will be less need to spend time keeping wealth in interest bearing assets.

    d. If there is wide spread severe deflation, there may also be threats to the stability of the system, in the same way that inflation caused these problems.

    e. Deflation may be very costly if nominal wages cannot fall. A deflation means that if there is no change in the nominal wage, the real wage will be rising – potentially causing additional unemployment. Just as inflation can grease the wheel of the labor market, deflation can throw in sand and create unemployment.

5. Natural rate of unemployment: alternative approach.

    a. First set $fU = sE$ and divide by L to get:

    $$f(U/L) = s(E/L).$$

    Since $E = L - U$,

    $$f(U/L) = s[(L - U) / L]$$
    $$f u = s (1 - u)$$
    $$f u + s u = s$$
    $$u (f + s) = s$$

    $$u = s / (f + s).$$

    b. This is the natural rate because at this rate, the number of people who find jobs will equal the number of people who lose jobs and hence the unemployment rate will not change. If the unemployment rate were higher than this natural rate, flows out of unemployment would exceed inflows, and the unemployment rate would fall. The reverse is true as well, so the economy tends towards the natural rate.

c.   If the separation rate, s, increases, the natural rate of unemployment will increase. (You can verify this if you wish by finding $\delta u/\delta s$ and showing that it is positive.)

d.   If the rate of jobs found, f, increases, the natural rate of unemployment will decrease.

e.   The same policies discussed in the textbook as affecting the natural rate will have the same impact in this model. In particular temp agencies will likely increase f. Policies or unions that make it more difficult to fire workers may decrease s. (But it also may affect f at the same time!)

CHAPTER 4

Multiple Choice

1. e. All of the above. The circular flow diagram includes the major macro markets as well as the households, firms, and the government.

2. b. The aggregate production function is of the form $Y = A \cdot F(K, L)$; where capital (K), and labor (L) are the factors of production.

3. b. Each successive unit is assumed to have less and less of an impact on output.

4. d. This is directly from definition of constant returns to scale. If you multiply the inputs by any given number, output will increase by the same amount, if the function has constant returns to scale.

5. c. The interest rate is the "cost" of investment. As the cost rises, fewer firms will invest. Firms also only care about the real interest rate. (Remember, "firms invest, people save.")

6. b. In the short-run, demand determines output.

7. d. In the long-run, supply determines output. Also, in the long-run supply is equal to potential output.

8. c. In the long-run, an increase in spending will have no impact on output. Consumption is not changed since income and taxes have not changed. Since $Y = C + I + G$, an increase in G must lead to a decline in investment.

9. a. Net investment = gross investment – depreciation.

10. a. The current account measures the goods and services side of the economy, while the capital account measures flows of financial assets.

True/False/Uncertain

1. False. Investment equals the sum of government savings, private savings, *and foreign savings.*

2. False/Uncertain. Since $Y = C + I + G + (X - M)$, exports can exceed production if imports are large.

3. False. In the long-run, an increase in spending will have no impact on output. Consumption will not change in the long-run (income and taxes have not changed). Since $Y = C + I + G$, an increase in G must lead to a decline in investment.

4. False. In the short-run government spending can impact income, and hence private savings. In the long-run government spending will have no impact on private savings.

5. True. If there were no diminishing marginal returns in any factor, then you could double output by doubling that one factor alone. So if you double all the factors, you would necessarily have more than twice the output.

For example, in the production function: $Y = K \, L^{0.5}$, capital does not have diminishing marginal returns since if you double K, you also double Y. Now if you double both K and L, output will increase by more than 2 times.

To summarize, if we assume more than one factor of production and positive marginal product: no diminishing returns will imply no constant returns to scale. Hence constant returns to scale implies diminishing returns.

Problems

1. Production functions:

   Constant returns to scale:

   a. $Y/L = 2\,K/L$; so $Y = 2\,K$. If we multiply both K and L by a constant, a:

   $$2\,aK = a(2K) = aY.$$

   b. $Y/L = (K/L)^{0.5}$; so $Y = (K/L)^{0.5}\,L = K^{0.5}L^{0.5}$. If we multiply both K and L by a constant, a:

   $$(aK)^{0.5}(aL)^{0.5} = a\,K^{0.5}L^{0.5} = a\,Y.$$

   c. $Y/L = (K/L)^{2}$; so $Y = (K/L)^{2}\,L = K^{2}(1/L)$. If we multiply both K and L by a constant, a:

   $$(aK)^{2}(1/aL) = a^{2}/a\,K^{2}(1/L) = a\,K^{2}(1/L) = a\,Y.$$

   So all three of these functions have constant returns to scale.

   Marginal product:

   a. This production function has constant marginal product of capital, and does not depend on labor.

   b. There is diminishing marginal product of both capital and labor

   c. There is increasing marginal product of capital, and a negative marginal product of labor.

2. Cobb-Douglas production function

   a. Yes, the function has constant returns to scale:

   $Y = K^{a}L^{(1-a)}$. If we multiply both K and L by a constant, c:

   $$(cK)^{a}(cL)^{(1-a)} = c^{a}\,c^{1-a}\,K^{a}L^{(1-a)} = c^{a+(1-a)}\,K^{a}L^{(1-a)} = c\,Y.$$

b. y $= Y/L = K^a L^{(1-a)} (1/L)$
       $= K^a L^{(1-a-1)}$
       $= K^a L^{(-a)}$
       $= K^a (1/L^a)$
       $= (K/L)^a$
       $= k^a$

c.   If a function $Y = F (K, L)$ has constant returns to scale then:

$$cY = F (cK, cL)$$

for any constant c. Consider the case where $c = 1/L$. In this case:

$(1/L)Y$ $= F[(1/L)K, (1/L)L]$
Y/L $= F (K/L, 1)$

The function F(K/L, 1), since 1 is simply a constant, can be written as a separate function $f(K/L)$, so

Y/L $= f(K/L),$ or
y $= f(k).$

3.   More production functions.

   a.   Increasing returns to scale, constant marginal product of both K and L.
   b.   Constant returns to scale, constant marginal product of both K and L.
   c.   Increasing returns to scale, constant marginal product of both K and L.
   d.   Constant returns to scale, diminishing marginal product of both K and L.
   e.   Constant returns to scale, diminishing marginal product of both K and L.
   f.   Increasing returns to scale, constant marginal product of K, diminishing returns to L.
   g.   Increasing returns to scale, diminishing marginal product of K, increasing returns to L.

4.   Marginal propensity to save.

If $C = 100 + 0.9 Y$, we can write the amount of savings as

S $= Y - C$
        $= Y - 100 + 0.9 Y$
        $= -100 + 0.1 Y.$

The mps is therefore 0.1

The general rule is that the *mps* = *1 – mpc*. So, the higher the marginal propensity to consume, the lower the marginal propensity to save.

5. Components of output.

    a. Private savings is $S = Yd - C = $ 9 trillion – 7 trillion = 2 trillion.

    b. Investment is the sum of private, government and foreign savings:

    $$I = S = S_p + S_g + S_f$$
    $$I = S = 2 + (-0.5) + 0 = 1.5 \; trillion$$

    c. Government spending is found by using the relation Y = C + I + G + (X - M).

    $$10 = 7 + 1.5 + G + 0.$$
    $$G = 1.5.$$

6. AS/AD (First pass).

    a. An increase in government spending will increase output in the short-run but will not affect prices. In the long-run, the shift will increase prices, but not output.

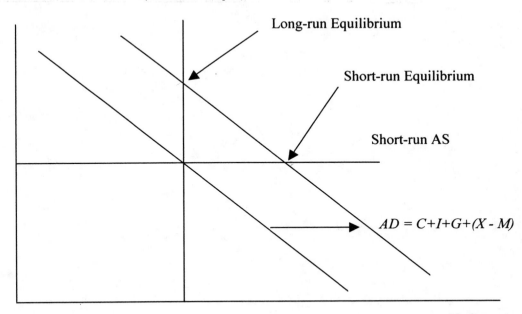

b. A decline in investment will decrease output in the short-run but will not affect prices. In the long-run, the shift will decrease prices, but not output.

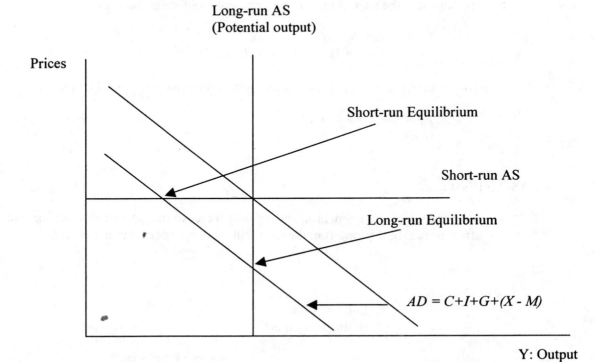

Chapter 5

Multiple Choice

1. e. At the beginning of the 1800's, the beginning of the industrial revolution, growth accelerated to about 0.2% per year, and eventually reached the relatively high levels of today.

2. d. Technology is assumed to be exogenous.

3. b. Investment will add to capital per person, while depreciation and population growth subtract. You can use the ln trick to find the rate of change of capital per person: $\%\Delta (K/L) = \%\Delta K - \%\Delta L$.

4. c. The capital stock per person will under certain conditions (steady state with no technology growth), be constant, but we do not assume this.

5. c. When $i = (n+d)\ k$ additions to capital offset reductions to capital, and balanced growth is achieved.

6. a. In the long-run, the increase in the savings rate will lead to an increase in the level of output, but not the rate of growth of output. So, in the short-run, there will be an increase in growth while the economy transitions to a new steady state.

7. a. In the long-run, the one-time increase in technology will lead to an increase in the level of output, but not the rate of growth of output. So, in the short-run, there will be an increase in growth while the economy transitions to a new steady state. Technology would have to be continually increasing in order to get a permanent long-run increase in output growth.

8. c. The steady state level of output per capita is constant, which implies that output must be growing at the same rate as population.

9. c. Only persistent technological change can cause steady state growth in the model.

10. e. If any of these factors are changed, output per person will change as well.

True/False/Uncertain

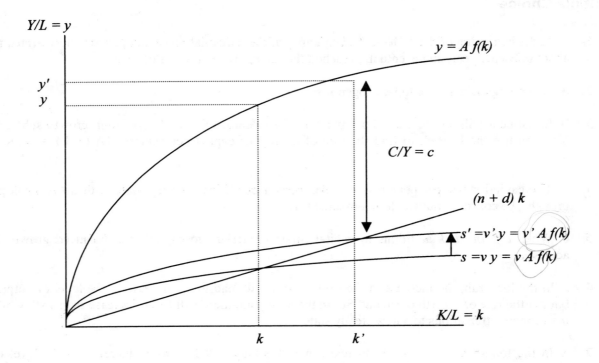

The diagram above shows an increase in the savings rate from v to v'.

For growth questions, you need to distinguish carefully between output (Y), output per capita (y), the rate of growth of output (%ΔY), and the rate of growth of output per capita (%Δy).

1. False. The greater savings rate will increase output per person, but not the long-run steady state *growth rate*.

2. True. As the savings rate increases, output per person will increase.

3. False. As the savings rate increases, output does increase which might lead to more consumption. However, by saving more people are consuming less of their income. The effect will depend upon whether the capital stock, before the savings change, was greater than or less than the *golden rule* level of capital.

4. True. In steady state, both output and capital will grow at the rate of population growth.

5. True. An increase in the population growth rate will rotate the (n + d) k line up, and hence lead to lower per capita output. In the long-run, once the economy returns to steady state, output will return to its steady state rate of growth which is now higher since population growth is higher.

Problems

1. Solow growth model.

    a. Savings rate increase.

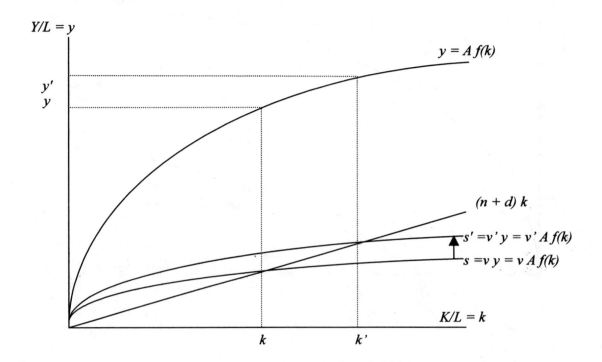

Steady state:	Output per person:	higher level
	Growth rate of output per person:	no change
Short-run:	Output per person:	begins to increase
	Growth rate of output per person:	increase

Output has increased in this scenario because a greater fraction of output is being devoted to investment and capital accumulation. Once the economy reaches the new steady state, however, the economy does not grow at a faster rate.

b. Depreciation rate decline.
    The steady state capital line *(n+d) k* will rotate downwards.

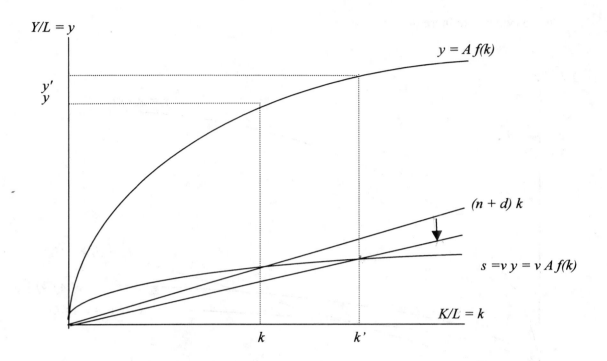

Steady state:	Output per person:	higher level
	Growth rate of output per person:	no change
Short-run:	Output per person:	begins to increase
	Growth rate of output per person:	temporary increase

A decline in the rate of depreciation means that less of the capital stock needs to be replaced each year. Therefore, the amount of capital that can be maintained in the steady state is higher. As in the precious case there is no change in the growth rate once the economy reaches the steady state.

c.   Increase in the population growth rate.

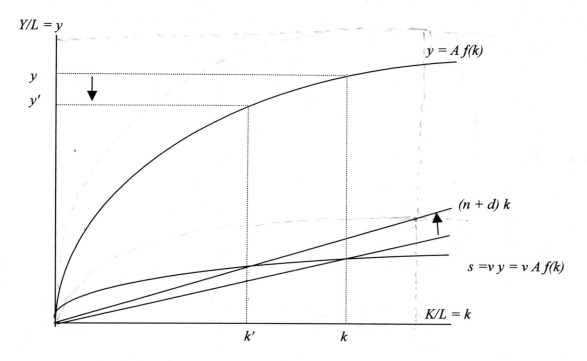

The steady state capital line *(n+d) k* will rotate upwards.

| Steady state: | Output per person: | lower level |
| | Growth rate of output per person: | no change |

| Short-run: | Output per person: | begins to decrease |
| | Growth rate of output per person: | begins to decrease (negative) |

A decline in the rate of depreciation means that less of the capital stock needs to be replaces each year. Therefore the amount of capital that can be maintained in the steady state is higher. As in the precious case there is no change in the growth rate once the economy reaches the steady state.

d.   One time increase in technology.
     The increase in technology will shift the $y = Af(k)$ curve upwards.

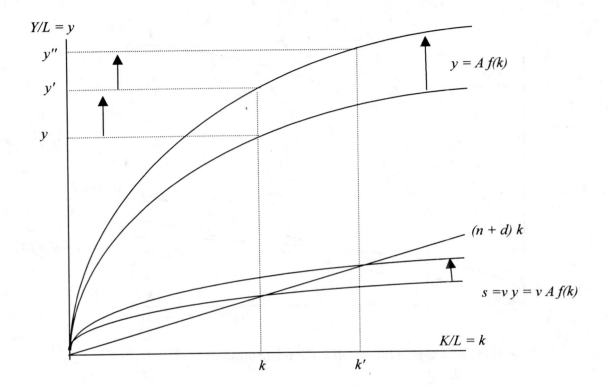

Steady state:	Output per person:	higher level
	Growth rate of output per person:	no change
Short-run:	Output per person:	immediate increase
	Growth rate of output per person:	temporary increase

A decline in the rate of depreciation means that less of the capital stock needs to be replaces each year. Therefore the amount of capital that can be maintained in the steady state is higher. As in the precious case there is no change in the growth rate once the economy reaches the steady state.

e.   Earthquake.
     The earthquake will immediately reduce the capital stock. Over time it will return to the previous steady state level.

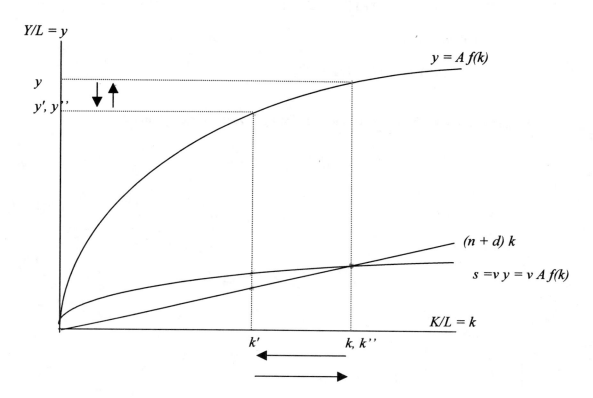

Steady state: Output per person: no change
                 Growth rate of output per person: no change

Short-run: Output per person: lower
                 Growth rate of output per person: temporary increase

The earthquake reduces the levels of capital and output per person immediately. The economy is now below the steady state, which means that the economy will increase its capital stock per person until it reached the pre-earthquake level.

2.   Solow growth: steady state.

     a. $y = k^{0.5}$.
     b.   Investment is given by i = v y, and, in steady state,
          $$i = (n + d)\,k\,,$$
          $$v\,k^{0.5} = (n + d)\,k,$$
          $$v\,/\,(n + d) = k\,/\,k^{0.5},$$
          $$v\,/\,(n + d) = k^{0.5}.$$

          Plugging in numbers, we get that: $k = 12\% / (1\% + 2\%) = 12/3 = 4$.
     c.   The steady state level of income per capital is therefore $y = k^{0.5} = 4^{0.5} = 2$.

    d. Since there is no steady state growth in per capita output, the rate of output growth equals the rate of growth of the population, which is 1%. This can be found by noting that:

$$\%\Delta(Y/L) = \%\Delta Y - \%\Delta L = 0,$$

and, therefore,

$$\%\Delta Y = \%\Delta L = 1\%.$$

3. The diagram below shows the economies for the two countries (1 and 2).

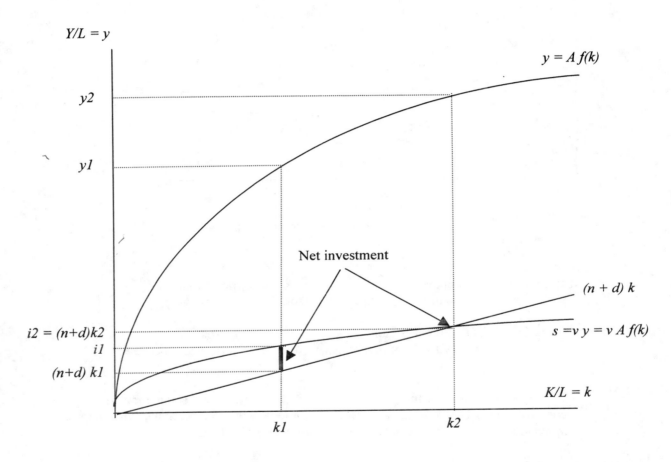

    a. See Diagram.
    b. See Diagram.
    c. For country 2, if there were no investment, capital would shrink at the level designated by $i2$ and is equal to $(n+d)\ k2$. For country 1, if there were no investment, capital would shrink by $(n+d)\ k1$.
    d. Net investment for country 2 is zero. Net investment for country 1 is shown in bold on the graph.
    e. In the short-run, country 1 will grow faster.
    f. In the steady state, both countries will grow at the same rate.

4. The diagram below shows the economies for the two countries (1 and 2).

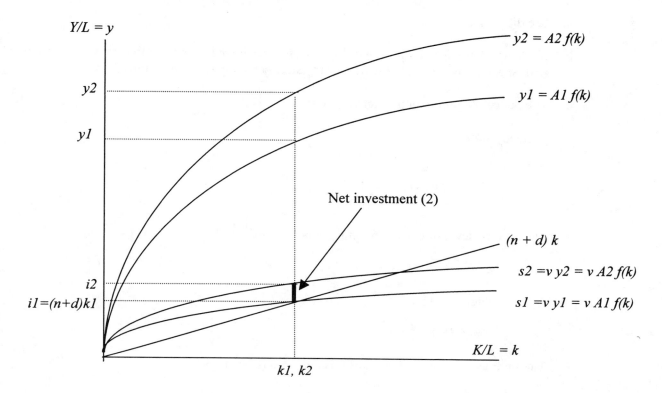

a. See diagram.

b. See diagram.

c. For country 1, if there were no investment, capital would shrink at the level designated by *i1* and is equal to *(n+d) k1*. For country 1, if there were no investment, capital would shrink by the same amount *(n+d) k2*. since *k1 = k2*.

d. Net investment for country 1 is zero. Net investment for country 2 is shown in bold on the graph.

e. In the short-run, country 2 will grow faster until it reaches the new steady state.

f. When both countries are at the new steady state, the growth rates will be equal. Country 2 will have a higher level of output, but the same growth rate.

5. The Golden Rule

    a. See diagram above.

    b. If savings were very high or very low, consumption would be very low as well. So there will be some savings rate at which steady state consumption is maximized.

    c. The per capita production function is $y = k^a$.

    d. In steady state,

$$\begin{aligned} c &= y - s \\ &= y - d\,k^{SS} \\ &= (k^{SS})^a - d\,k^{SS}. \end{aligned}$$

    e. The optimal level of consumption is found at $\delta c / \delta k^{SS} = 0$.

$$\delta c / \delta k^{SS} = a(k^{SS})^{a-1} - d = 0,$$

which solves to:

$$k^{SS} = (d/a)^{1/(a-1)}.$$

    f. The savings rate that will achieve this outcome is given by

$$\begin{aligned} v\,Y &= d\,k^{SS} \\ v\,(k^{SS})^a &= d\,k^{SS} \\ v &= d\,(k^{SS})^{1-a}. \end{aligned}$$

CHAPTER 6

Multiple Choice

1. b. For countries with similar characteristics, poorer countries will transition towards the steady state equilibrium faster than will richer countries.

2. d. The model predicts that as countries get close to their steady state, growth rates should decline. Empirically, growth rates appear to have accelerated over the past 200 years.

3. d. The other factors are components of the new growth theory, but technology is the main focus.

4. d. Increasing returns implies that the marginal product of capital is not necessarily diminishing, and so any of these outcomes may result.

5. b. The other answers may lead to productivity increases as well, but learning by doing is the idea that as one produces a good, one becomes better at production.

6. d. Shumpeter's view of the economy emphasized innovation, the people who develop innovation, as well as the process by which the economy rewards good innovations and punishes old technology.

7. b. Empirically labor force growth is the largest determinant of output (46%); and technology is the largest component of output per person.

    The growth accounting equation:

    $$\%\Delta Y = \%\Delta A + 0.3\%\Delta K + 0.7\%\Delta L.$$

    Empirically,

    $$\%\Delta A = 1.1\,\%,$$
    $$\%\Delta K = 4.0\,\%,$$
    $$\%\Delta L. = 1.0\,\%.$$

8. d. Any of these factors can affect growth rates across countries.

9. c. Parts (a) and (b) are true of both models. Part (d) is true only of Solow growth theory. New growth theory predicts that the savings rate may affect the long-run rate of growth in the economy.

10. a. Technological innovation often depends on what came before it. So to really understand the detail of innovation, you often have to look to see what happened in the past.

True/False/Uncertain

1. False. Growth rates have tended to accelerate over this time period from about 0.5% in the early 1800s to just over 2% in the most recent period.

2. False. The Solow growth model predicts that two countries *with similar characteristics* will tend to converge to the same steady-state level of output per capita. The characteristics that will affect the level of output per capita in the Solow growth model are population growth, depreciation rate, savings rate, and technology.

3. False. The data does not show a very clear relation, and there are examples of cases where high savings does not lead to higher growth.

4. False. It is very difficult to measure technological growth directly. It can be measured as a residual however. Remember the growth accounting relationship:

$$\%\Delta Y = \%\Delta A + 0.3\%\Delta K + 0.7\%\Delta L.$$

We can rewrite this as:

$$\%\Delta A = \%\Delta Y - 0.3\%\Delta K - 0.7\%\Delta L.$$

Then, by measuring $\%\Delta Y$, $\%\Delta K$, and $\%\Delta L$, we can find the growth rate of technology. This measure of technology growth is the Solow residual.

5. False. Patents do create a monopoly; so, they do create some efficiency loss. However, the profit that is generated by the creation of that monopoly creates an incentive to innovate, and to develop new technology.

6. Uncertain. Technology, like other goods, can be "produced" by devoting resources to its production. However, it is difficult to predict or accurately control when technological innovations are made. In addition, there is the issue of path dependence in the creation of technology.

Problems

1. The growth accounting relation for the production function given is:

$$\%\Delta Y = \%\Delta A + 0.7\%\Delta L + 0.3\,\%\Delta K$$

   a. The rate of growth of output is therefore: $\%\Delta Y = 2 + 0.7(1) + 0.3(3) = 3.6\%$.
   b. The rate of growth of output per person is $\%\Delta(Y/L) = \%\Delta Y - \%\Delta L = 3.6 - 1 = 2.6$.

2. The growth accounting equation for the U.S. is:

$$\%\Delta Y = \%\Delta A + 0.7\%\Delta L + 0.3\,\%\Delta K$$

So $\%\Delta A = \%\Delta Y - 0.7\%\Delta L - \%\Delta K = 2.5 - 0.7(1) - 0.3(3) = 0.9$

3. Non-diminishing returns.

    a. Yes, this function has constant returns to scale.
    b. No, this function does not have diminishing marginal product. It has constant marginal product since if you multiply capital by any given amount, output will increase by the same multiple.

    c. $\%\Delta Y = \%\Delta A + \%\Delta K$.
    d. In each period the capital stock will tend to increase by $v\,Y = v\,A\,K$.
    e. In each period the capital stock will tend to decrease by $d\,K$.
    f. In each period the capital stock will on net grow by

$$\Delta K = v\,A\,K - d\,K.$$

The growth rate is then

$$\%\Delta K = \Delta K / K = v\,A - d.$$

This number may be greater than or less than zero. Note that it does not depend on the capital stock.

    g. The growth rate of output is then the same as in (f), $\%\Delta Y = vA - d$.
    h. See diagram below.

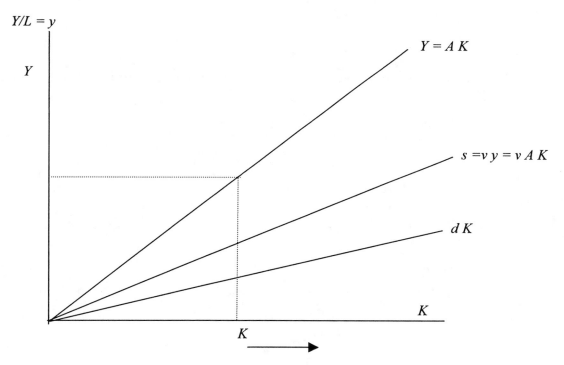

    i. If $vA > d$, the savings line will be above the depreciation line and the economy will continue to grow.

    j.   These results differ from the Solow model in that a) growth can continue forever and need not slow down to the rate of population growth; b) it is possible for countries to continue to contract even in the long-run, and c) the growth rate of output in the long-run depends upon the savings rate.

4. Skilled labor.

It will help to write out the growth accounting equation for this production function.

$$\%\Delta Y = \%\Delta A + 0.2\,\%\Delta LL + 0.6\,\%\Delta LH + 0.3\,\%\Delta K.$$

    a.   If LH increases by 100% (doubles), then Y will increase by 20%.

    b.   If LH increases by 100% (doubles), then Y will increase by 60%.

    c.   If 2% of the population was trained, $\%\Delta LL = -4\%$ and $\%\Delta LH = +4\%$. This means that output will grow by $0.2\,(-4) + 0.6\,(4) = 1.6\%$

    d.   The following year, 2% of the population will be more than four percent of the low skilled workers. It will also be less than 4 percent of the skilled workers. This means that output will grow by less than 1.6%. In fact, every year will see a further decline in the growth increases from additional training.

    e.   The production function is:

$$Y = A\,LL^{0.2}\,LH^{0.6}\,K^{0.3}$$

Note that the entire population is either skilled or unskilled so L = LH + LL, or LL=L-LH, so:

$$Y = A\,(L - LH)^{0.2}\,LH^{0.6}\,K^{0.3}$$

$$dy/dLH = A\,K^{0.3}\,[0.6\,LH^{0.4}\,(L-LH)^{0.2}\,L - 0.2(L-LH)^{-0.8}\,LH^{0.6}] = 0.$$
$$[0.6\,LH^{0.4}\,(L-LH)^{0.2}\,L - 0.2(L-LH)^{-0.8}\,LH^{0.6}] = 0$$
$$0.6\,LH^{0.4}\,(L-LH)^{0.2}\,L = 0.2(L-LH)^{-0.8}\,LH^{0.6}$$
$$3\,(L - LH) = LH$$
$$3L - 3LH = LH$$
$$3L = 4LH$$
$$LH = \tfrac{3}{4}\,L$$

So, the output-maximizing split is to have 75% of the population high skilled, and the other 25% low skilled.

Chapter 7

Multiple Choice

1. d. Money does not necessarily have to have value as a commodity. Flat money (such as paper currency) tends to have little or no intrinsic value.

2. d. Virtually all measures of money including M1, M2, etc, include all of these assets.

3. d. Unemployment, and output are assumed to be determined by the supply side of the economy, and velocity is assumed to be constant. Changes in money growth is then the primary force that drives changes in prices according to the quantity equation:

    $$M * V = P * Y.$$

4. d. The amount of the tax is given by the value of the money less the cost of producing it. The tax comes from the fact that inflation will reduce the purchasing power of consumers.

5. b. The long-run dichotomy separates the analysis of the real sector and the nominal sector. The quantity equation embodies this idea: output is determined by supply and hence the factors of production; while prices are determined by the money supply.

6. c. The U.S. exchange rate (with most countries) is allowed to fluctuate and is thus determined in the market. However, there are some countries (such as Argentina) that have fixed the value of their currency to the U.S. dollar. In addition, the government may occasionally intervene in the currency market to attempt to alter the value of the exchange rate with one or more countries.

7. b. The sum of the current account and the capital account must sum to zero. However, the sum of the current account and the private capital account can be out of balance if there is an intervention by the government in the market that result in official reserve transactions.

    Current account + Capital account =
    Current account + (Private capital account + Official reserve transactions) = 0.

8. b. The real exchange rate for the U.S. is given by

    $$ER = E \times (P_{U.S.} / P_{foreign}.)$$

    If E is fixed, then an increase in US prices or a decline in foreign prices would increase the real exchange rate. (The nominal exchange rate is given as foreign currency per dollar).

9. e. The law of one price translated to an international context implies purchasing power parity, and that the real exchange rate will equal one.

10. d. A balance of payments deficit implies that there is more supply of the currency than there is demand, so, to restore balance, the value of the currency must change.

True/False/Uncertain

1. False. According to the quantity equation:

$$M V = P Y, \text{ and hence}$$

$$\%\Delta M + \%\Delta V = \%\Delta P + \%\Delta Y.$$

So the rate of inflation will equal:

$$\%\Delta P = \%\Delta M + \%\Delta V - \%\Delta Y.$$

We assume that velocity is constant $\%\Delta V = 0$, but it may be the case that there is some real growth in the economy, so $\%\Delta Y$ is not necessarily equal to zero. In this case, inflation will not equal money growth. However, the *change* in the inflation rate will equal the *change* in the rate of growth of money supply.

2. True. As we move from M1 to M2 to M3, etc, the assets that are included are less and less liquid—that is, they are not as easily converted into assets that can be used for transactions. For example, savings deposits are not included in M1, but they are included in M2.

3. False. The evidence shows a positive relationship between money growth and inflation, but the relationship is not as close as the theory would suggest. In particular, when inflation is low, the quantity theory does not always do a good job of explaining inflation

4. False. The current account equals the negative of the capital account.

5. True. If the fixed exchange rate happens to be exactly at the free market exchange rate, then there would be no intervention required. If, however, the fixed exchange rate is at a different level, official reserve purchases or sales would be necessary to prevent the exchange rate from adjusting to the equilibrium.

Problems

1. The current account must equal the negative of the capital account.

> Current account balance is primarily: (exports – imports)
> Private capital account balance: (inflows – outflows) of financial capital

If exchange rates are flexible, there are no official transactions, and so the capital account is $100 billion minus $60 billion, which equals $40 billion. This implies that the current account balance is a deficit of $40 billion.

2. Since we want to consider the long-run we should use the quantity equation:

$$M\,V = P\,Y$$

Which translates to

$$\%\Delta M + \%\Delta\,V = \%\Delta\,P + \%\Delta\,Y,\text{ and hence}$$
$$\%\Delta M = \%\Delta\,P + \%\Delta\,Y - \%\Delta\,V.$$

a. According to the quantity theory $\%\Delta V = 0$. So the Fed should set the money supply to equal:
$$\%\Delta M = 2\% + 2.5\% = 4.5\%.$$

b. If the velocity of money is not equal to zero, the Fed should set $\%\Delta M = 4.5 - \%\Delta\,V$. The Fed must make some forecast of the change in velocity in order to correctly set the money supply.

c. If they follow the policy in part (a) inflation may be different from 2%. If velocity unexpectedly increased, this would meant that prices would rise more than desired.

3. Again using the quantity equation:

$$\%\Delta M + \%\Delta\,V = \%\Delta\,P + \%\Delta\,Y$$

a. Inflation will be 6% - 2% = 4%.
b. Nominal GDP will grow at a rate of 2% + 4% = 6%.
c. If the money supply grew to 8%, inflation would also increase by 2 percentage points to 6%. There will be no change in real GDP in the long-run, and nominal GDP growth will also increase by 2 percentage points to reach 8%.

4. If purchasing power parity holds and the exchange rate is flexible, the nominal exchange rate will change when inflation changes.

$$ER = E\,P^{US} / P^{foreign}.$$

With PPP, ER = 1, so

$$E = P^{foreign} / P^{US}$$

If prices double in the U.S., the exchange rate will fall to half its previous value, and hence would decrease in value relative to other currencies in the world.

5.   Inflation and exchange rates.

    a.   Since:

$$ER = E\, P^{US} / P^{foreign}.$$

And hence

$$\%\Delta ER = \%\Delta E + \%\Delta P^{US} - \%\Delta P^{foreign}.$$

If nominal exchange rates as fixed $\%\Delta E = 0$, we get that

$$\%\Delta ER = \%\Delta E + \%\Delta P^{US} - \%\Delta P^{foreign}.$$

    b.   If PPP holds, the real exchange rate is fixed (because of the law of one price), hence:

$$0 = \%\Delta ER = \%\Delta E + \%\Delta P^{US} - \%\Delta P^{foreign}.$$
$$\%\Delta E = \%\Delta P^{foreign} - \%\Delta P^{US}.$$

Chapter 8

Multiple Choice

1. a. In the short-run, prices are assumed to be fixed, and demand determined output (Hansen's Law). In the long-run we will allow prices to adjust.

2. e. The multiplier model assumes the aggregate expenditures will be:

    $AE = C + I + G + (X - M)$.

3. d. The multiplier model assumes that consumption is given by:

    Consumption: $C = C_0 + mpc(Y - T)$.

    Substituting into the AE equation and solving for Y gives:

    $Y = [1/(1-mpc)] [C_0 - mpc(T_0) + I_0 + G_0 + (X_0 - M_0)]$.

4. c. The IS curve comes from the multiplier model and represents equilibrium in the goods market. The LM curve comes from the supply and demand for money market and represents equilibrium in the money market.

5. c. The IS curve is downward sloping and related to interest rates and output. The negative slope comes from the fact that higher interest rates tend to lower investment.

6. b. The IS curve shows what happens when you allow investment to depend on the interest rate.

7. e. Since the IS curve comes from the multiplier model in which $Y = C + I + G + (X - M)$ autonomous changes in any of these factors will shift the IS curve.

8. d. The Fed controls the supply of money, not the demand.

9. b. A change in the interest rates will move you *along* the money demand curve, but will not shift the entire curve. All of these factors will cause the *quantity* of money demanded to change.

10. b. The authority to control the money supply lies in the hands of the Fed. Bank behavior is able to impact the money supply through their lending practices, but the Fed can always adjust to compensate.

True/False/Uncertain

1. False. An increase will shift the curve to the *right*, leading to *higher output* and lower *interest rates*. See the graph below.

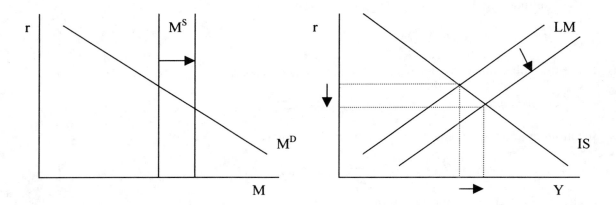

2. True. An increase in G will shift the IS curve out, leading to higher interest rates and lower investment. See the following graph.

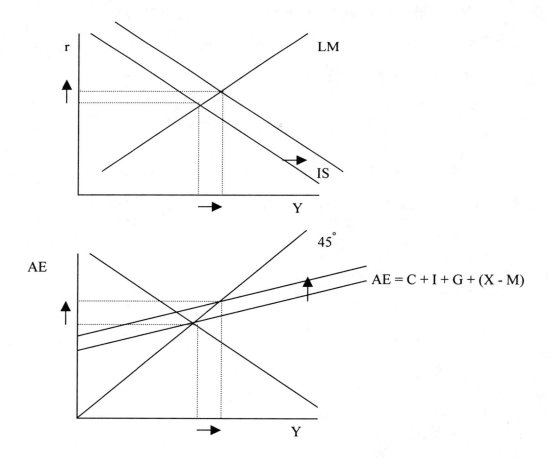

3. False. If investment is very sensitive to interest rates, then a small interest rate change will lead to a large change in investment and therefore output. This implies that the curve will be relatively flat.

4. False. If the demand for money is very sensitive to changes in income, then a small change in income will lead to a large change in interest rates. This implies that the curve will then be relatively steep.

5. False. Fiscal policy shifts the IS curve by shifting the AE curve. Monetary policy can shift the LM curve by changing the money supply.

Problems

1. Balanced budget multiplier.

   a. By setting $Y = AE$ we get

   $$Y = C_0 + mpc(Y - T_0) + I_0 + G_0 + (X_0 - M_0).$$
   $$Y = 1/(1-mpc) [C_0 - mpc(T_0) + I_0 + G_0 + (X_0 - M_0)].$$

   Putting in the numbers this gives:

   $$Y = 1/(1-0.9) [100 - 0.9(100) + 200 + 100 + 0]$$
   $$= 10 [310]$$
   $$= 3,100.$$

   b. If government spending becomes 200, then

   $$Y = 1/(1-0.9) [100 - 0.9(100) + 200 + 200 + 0]$$
   $$= 10 [410]$$
   $$= 4,100.$$

   Output has increased by 1,000.

   c. The government spending multiplier is therefore $\Delta Y/\Delta G = \$1,000 / \$100 = 10$.

   d. The budget was balanced before the increase in expenditures. Now the budget balance is $T - G = 100 - 200 = -100$. So there is a budget deficit of 100.

   e. If both T and G are equal to 200, then

   $$Y = 1/(1-0.9) [100 - 0.9(200) + 200 + 200 + 0]$$
   $$= 10 [320]$$
   $$= 3,200$$

   f. Equilibrium in this case has increased by 100. The government spending multiplier when taxes adjusted by the same amount is therefore $\Delta Y/\Delta G = \$100 / \$100 = 1$.

g. Start with the equilibrium output equation from above,

$$Y = 1/(1\text{-}mpc) [C_0 - mpc(T_0) + I_0 + G_0 + (X_0 - M_0)].$$

If taxes are always equal to government spending, $T = G$, we can substitute out T_0 in the equation to get

$$Y = 1/(1\text{-}mpc) [C_0 - mpc(G_0) + I_0 + G_0 + (X_0 - M_0)],.$$
$$Y = 1/(1\text{-}mpc) [C_0 + I_0 + G_0 (1 - mpc) + (X_0 - M_0)],$$
$$Y = 1/(1\text{-}mpc) [G_0 (1 - mpc)] + 1/(1\text{-}mpc) [C_0 + I_0 + (X_0 - M_0)],$$
$$Y = G_0 + 1/(1\text{-}mpc) [C_0 + I_0 + (X_0 - M_0)],$$

Therefore $\Delta Y = \Delta G_0$, and the "balanced budget multiplier" is equal to $\Delta Y / \Delta G_0 = 1$.

2. Fiscal policy.

   a. Since equilibrium output was 3,100 in the previous question, a 10% increase would mean we wanted to increase output by 310. Since the multiplier was 10, we would have to increase government spending by only 31.

   b. If both government spending and taxes were to increase (to keep the deficit from increasing), a increase of 310 would be necessary to boost output by the same amount.

3. The equilibrium level of output is found by

$$Y = 1/(1\text{-}mpc) [C_0 - mpc(T_0) + I_0 + G_0 + (X_0 - M_0)].$$

   a. Given the numbers in the problem, this means:

$$Y = 1/(1\text{-}0.8) [100 - 0.8(100) + 50 + 130 + 0].$$
$$Y = 5 [200]$$
$$Y = 1,000.$$

   b. Private savings is $Y - C = 1,000 - (100 + 0.8(1,000 - 100)) = 180$.

   c. The budget deficit is $G - T = 130 - 100 = 30$.

   d. Total savings   = private savings + government savings + foreign savings
      = 180 + (-30) + 0
      = 150
      = I.

   e. Equilibrium output is now lower by $1/(1\text{-}mpc) [\Delta C_0] = 5 (100\text{-}50) = 250$.

$$Y = 1/(1\text{-}0.8) [50 - 0.8(100) + 50 + 130 + 0].$$
$$Y = 5 [150]$$
$$Y = 750.$$

   f. Private savings is $Y - C = 750 - (50 + 0.8(750 - 100)) = 180$.

g. Even though people are trying to save more, the actual amount of money that is saved remains unchanged at 180! This is because when people try to save more in this model, output declines as a result, thus lowering income and reducing savings. Note that the private savings rate, S/(Y – T), does increase; but the absolute number of dollars remains the same.

h. In the long-run output returns to potential, so the levels of savings will increase, and there will be no paradox. Note that when the economy returns to potential, savings is higher, thus investment will be higher as well.

4. Money demand (LM)

   a. If $Y = 100$ the money demand function becomes

$$M^D = 1000 - 1000\, r + 10(100).$$
$$M^D = 2000 - 1000\, r.$$

See graph below.

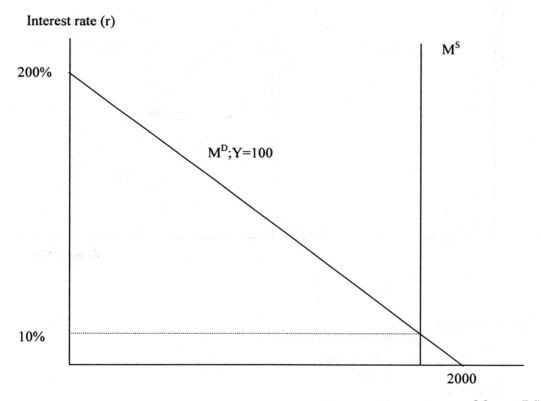

b. Equilibrium is found by setting supply equal to demand: $M^s = M^D$.

$$1900 = 2000 - 1000\,r$$
$$r = 100 / 1000$$
$$= 0.1 \text{ or } 10\%$$

c. See diagram below. An increase in income will shift the money demand curve to the right and cause a higher equilibrium interest rate.

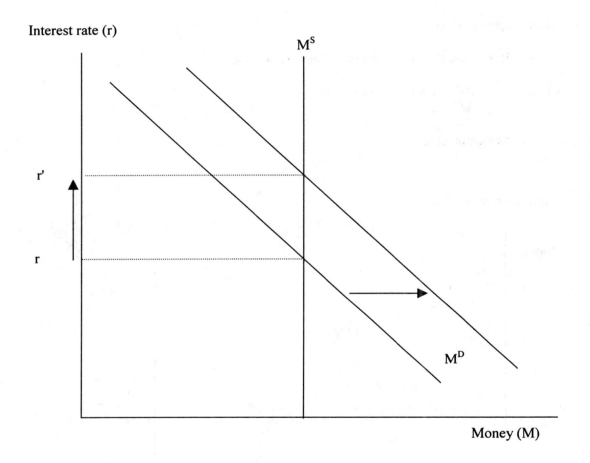

d. If $Y = 110$:
$$1900 = 2100 - 1000\,r$$
$$r = 200 / 1000$$
$$= 0.2 \text{ or } 20\%$$
If $Y = 120$:
$$1900 = 2200 - 1000\,r$$
$$r = 300 / 1000$$
$$= 0.3 \text{ or } 30\%$$

e.   See graph below.

Interest rate (r)

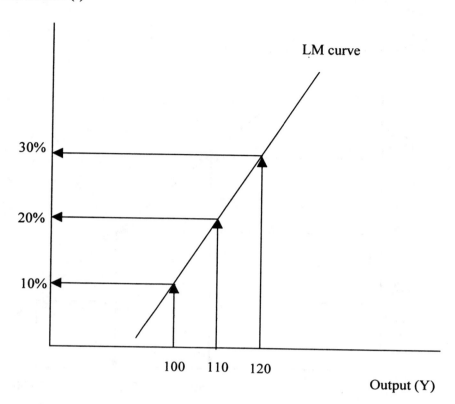

5.   Equilibrium output is again determined by

$$Y = 1/(1\text{-}mpc) \, [C_0 - mpc(T_0) + I + G_0 + (X_0 - M_0)].$$

Substituting in numbers:

$$Y = 1/(1\text{-}0.9) \, [100 - 0.9 \, (100) + I + 100 + 0].$$
$$Y = 10 \, [110 + I]$$

a.   If $r = 0.05$: $I = 200 - 1000 \, (0.05) = 150.$
      And therefore, $Y = 10 \, [110 + 150] = 2,600$

      If $r = 0.10$: $I = 200 - 1000 \, (0.10) = 100.$
      And therefore, $Y = 10 \, [110 + 100] = 2,100$

      If $r = 0.15$: $I = 200 - 1000 \, (0.15) = 50.$
      And therefore, $Y = 10 \, [110 + 50] = 1,600$

b. See the graph below.

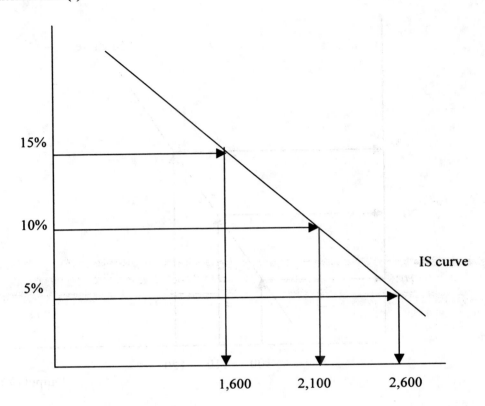

Chapter 9

Multiple Choice

You may find the IS/LM graph below useful in following the answers.

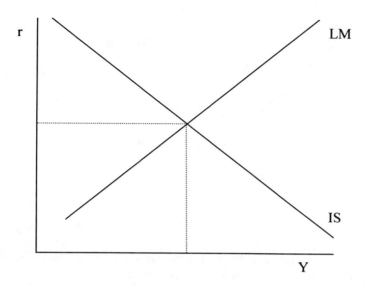

1. b. Fiscal policy affects government spending and/or taxation, so it shifts the IS curve. The aim of expansionary policy is to increase output, so the curve shifts to the right.

2. d. Fiscal policy affects the money supply, so it shifts the LM curve. The aim of expansionary policy is to increase output, so the curve shifts to the right.

3. c. The increase in spending shifts the IS to the right increasing output and increasing interest rates. The higher interest rates cause investment to decline.

4. c. Both risk and maturity differences can cause interest rates to differ. Interest rates will be the same on various assets only if they share the same risk and maturity characteristics.

5. a. The *structural* budget deficit would take out the effects of the state of the economy by giving the deficit that would exist if the economy were at potential output. The structural budget deficit would be a better indicator of the stance of policy. The cyclical budget deficit shows the component of the deficit that is related to the state of the economy.

6. d. Each of these factors makes policy difficult.

7. c. Accommodative policy will shift to the right both the IS and the LM curves leading to higher output and (if properly coordinated) little or no change in interest rates.

8. d. The yield curve usually shows that bonds with longer maturities pay higher interest rates. The opposite is true when the yield curve is inverted.

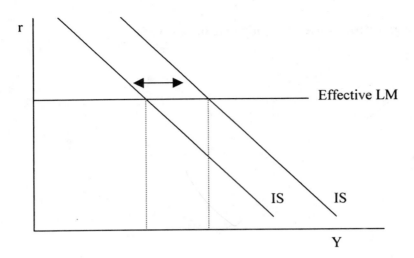

9. a. The effective LM curve is horizontal and located at the targeted interest rate (see graph). In this case, any shift in the IS curve will have a large impact on output.

10. e. If the Fed wishes to keep output unchanged, it will move the LM curve so as to keep Y constant. This is similar to the previous question, except that the "effective LM curve" is now vertical (see graph). A shift in the IS curve then leads to higher interest rates and hence lower investment. It will also lead to a deficit since government spending is unchanged. Since income is unchanged, and taxes are lower; consumption will increase since:

$$C = C_0 + mpc \ (Y - T).$$

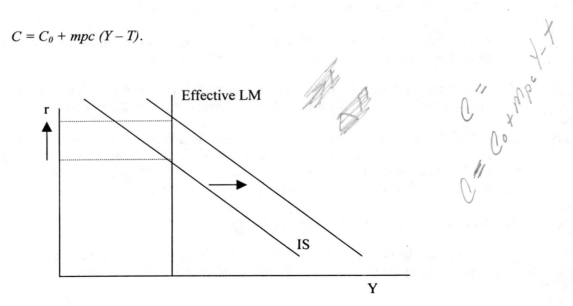

True/False/Uncertain

1. False. There are two reasons why this might not be the case: 1) the multiplier, and 2) the crowding out effect. The multiplier: 1/(1-mpc) will cause output to increase more than the $100 increase in G. The crowding out effect is caused by the higher interest that results from the increase in the IS curve. The higher interest rates will lower investment and hence will tend to decrease output.

2. False. The decline in the money supply will lead to higher interest rates and thus *lower* investment. This is represented by a shift to the left of the LM curve.

3. Uncertain. The budget surplus is the combination of the cyclical surplus (the surplus due to the economy operating above potential) and the structural surplus (the surplus due to policy actions). So the answer depends upon whether or not the structural surplus is greater than or less than zero.

4. True. Ricardian equivalence notes that when the government increases its debt, it must eventually pay it back. If people realize this and take it into account when they make decisions about how much to consume and save, a debt increase will be met by a decline in consumption (because people will increase savings in order to pay *future* taxes) in the same amount as an immediate tax increase.

5. False. Because of the slow political process, fiscal policy is thought to have long delays. In practice, the Fed has been much quicker to react to economic conditions.

6. False. A government spending increase will lead to an increase in output through a shift in the IS curve. This leads to higher interest rates and lower investment.

The reason why interest rates are higher is precisely *because* of the output increase. If investment were to have declined more than the increase in government spending, output would have declined, and interest rates would be lower than where they started. This cannot be the case since lower interest rates imply higher investment.

Problems

1. Short-run impacts of shocks using IS/LM. In each of the following, investment will move in the opposite direction as interest rates since $I = I(r)$ in the IS/LM model.

    a. Decrease in taxes.

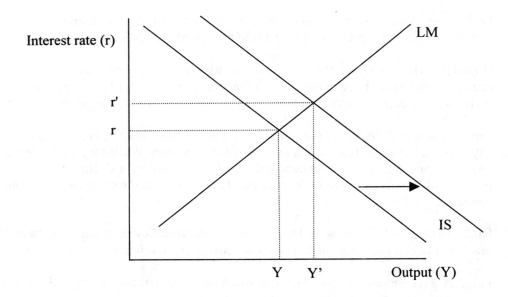

The tax reduction leads to a higher level of output at each level of interest rates, and hence a shift to the right of the IS curve. Output: Increase; Interest rates: Increase Investment: Decrease; Consumption: Increase.

b. Increase in money supply.

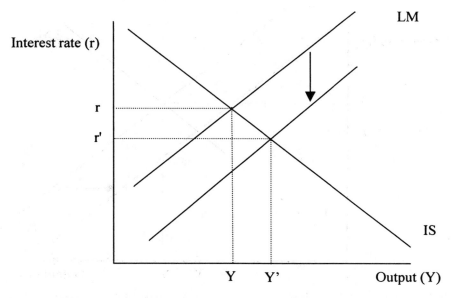

The increase in the money supply will lower interest rates at each level of output, and will result in a shift downward in the LM curve. Output: Increase; Interest rates: Decrease; Investment: Increase; Consumption: Increase

c. Both (a) and (b).

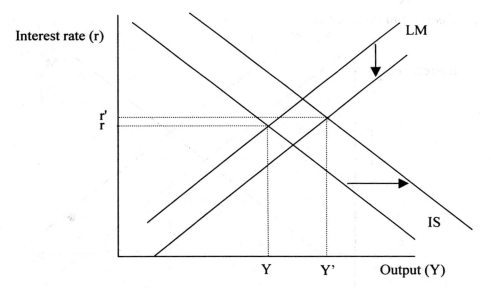

Note that the interest rate may increase, decrease, or remain unchanged. The direction of the change will depend upon the size of the shifts as well as the shapes of the IS and LM curves. The diagram shows the case where the interest rate rises. Output: Increase; Interest rates: Uncertain, may increase or decrease; Investment: Uncertain, may increase or decrease; Consumption: Increase.

d. Decline in exports.

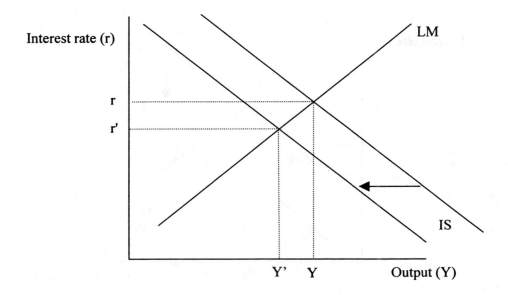

The decline in exports will lead to a decline in net exports $(X - M)$ and hence a drop in output at each level of interest rates, and hence shift left in the IS curve. Output: Decrease; Interest rates: Decrease; Investment: Increase; Consumption: Decrease.

e. Decrease in savings rate.

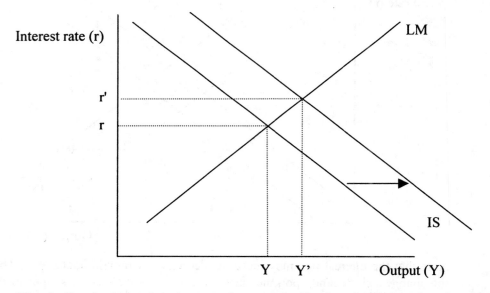

The decline in the savings rate can be a result of a drop in C_0 or a drop in *mpc* (or both). Either one will shift the IS curve to the right as in part (a). Output: Increase; Interest rates: Increase; Investment: Decrease; Consumption: Increase.

2. IS/LM with numbers. As usual, equilibrium is given by setting Y = AE and solving for Y. In this case, this yields the following equation for equilibrium output.

$$Y = 1/(1\text{-}mpc)\ [C_0 - mpc(T_0) + (I_0 - 1000\ r) + G_0 + (X_0 - M_0)].$$

a. Plugging in numbers we get that

$$\begin{aligned} Y &= 10\ [\ 100 - 0.9(100) + (300 - 100) + 100 + 0] \\ &= 10\ [\ 310\ ] \\ &= 3{,}100 \end{aligned}$$

b. If government spending increases, and there is no change in interest rates, output will drop by

$$\Delta Y = 1/(1\text{-}mpc)\ [\Delta G] = 10\ [100] = 1{,}000.$$

So output will increase by 1,000 to 4,100. ✓

c. On the IS/LM diagram, this means that the IS curve will shift to the right by 1,000. See below

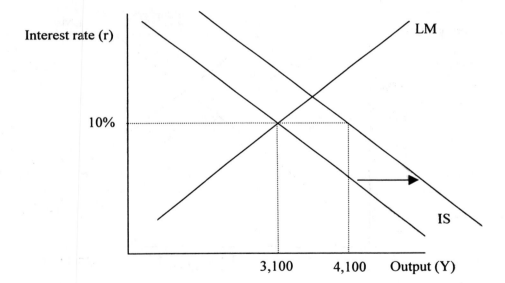

d. The new equilibrium output if interest rates increased to 15% will be found as follows:

$$Y = 10 [100 - 0.9(100) + (300 - 150) + 200 + 0]$$
$$= 10 [360]$$
$$= 3,600$$

Alternatively, we could note that an increase in interest rates will cause a reduction in investment of

$$\Delta I = \Delta(300 - 1,000r) = -1,000 \, \Delta r = -1,000 \, (0.05) = -50.$$

And then,

$$\Delta G = 1/(1-mpc) \, \Delta I,$$
$$= 10 [-50]$$
$$= -500.$$

This then is the reduction from 4,100 to 3,600. This new equilibrium is show in the following diagram

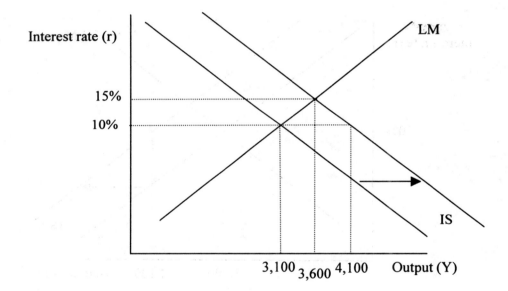

e. The net effect of the government spending increase was an increase in output of 500, and a decrease in investment of 50.

f. The magnitude of the effect will depend upon the multipliers as well as the shapes of the IS and LM curves. For example, if investment is very sensitive to interest rates (IS flat), or if interest rates are very sensitive to output increases (LM steep), the net change in output will be relatively small.

3. If fiscal policy is used to fight recessions, then when there is an economic downturn the government will either lower taxes or increase spending. This shifts the IS curve out. If fiscal policy does not react to expansions by shifting the IS curve to the left, then over the course of many business cycles the IS curve will continue to shift to the right (and will not tend to move back to the left).

    If monetary policy is used to fight both recessions and expansions, the LM curve will shift either up or down depending upon the state of the economy. Over time, the Fed will have to react more strongly to expansions since fiscal policy is not used, so over the course of many recessions, the LM curve will tend to move up.

    The Net effect of fiscal and monetary policy behaving this way will be greater interest rates, output and consumption at the same amount (if policymakers are successful), lower investment, and a greater budget deficit.

4. Balanced budget amendment.

    a. Equilibrium is given by setting $Y = AE$

    $$Y = C_0 + mpc(Y - T) + I_0 + G_0 + (X_0 - M_0)].$$

    Substituting for the tax $T = T_0 + tY$.

    $$
    \begin{aligned}
    Y &= C_0 - mpc[Y - (T_0 + tY)] + I_0 + G_0 + (X_0 - M_0), \\
    Y &= C_0 - mpc[Y - T_0 - tY)] + I_0 + G_0 + (X_0 - M_0), \\
    Y &= C_0 - mpc[Y(1-t) - T_0)] + I_0 + G_0 + (X_0 - M_0), \\
    Y &= C_0 - mpc(T_0) - mpcY(1-t) + I_0 + G_0 + (X_0 - M_0), \\
    Y + mpcY(1-t) &= C_0 - mpc(T_0) + I_0 + G_0 + (X_0 - M_0), \\
    Y(1+mpc(1-t)) &= C_0 - mpc(T_0) + I_0 + G_0 + (X_0 - M_0), \\
    \end{aligned}
    $$

    $$Y = 1/[1-mpc(1-t)] \times [C_0 - mpc(T_0) + I_0 + G_0 + (X_0 - M_0)],$$

    b. The multipliers is now $1/[1-mpc(1-t)]$.

    c. A $100 decrease in investment will lead to a change in output of:

    $$
    \begin{aligned}
    1/[1-mpc(1-t)] [-\$100] &= 1/[1-0.9(1-0.2)] [-\$100] \\
    &= 3.57 [-\$100] \\
    &= -\$357.
    \end{aligned}
    $$

    d. Income taxes are called automatic stabilizers because they reduce the sensitivity of output to autonomous changes in the economy by reducing the multiplier. When output is high, taxes will automatically increase, and vice versa, thus helping to stabilize the economy.

5. In order to keep output constant and increase investment, fiscal and monetary policymakers would have to coordinate their policies. Expansionary monetary policy and contractionary fiscal policy would lead to a reduction in interest rates, and hence an increase in investment, without affecting output (assuming the amount of the changes were precisely correct). See diagram below.

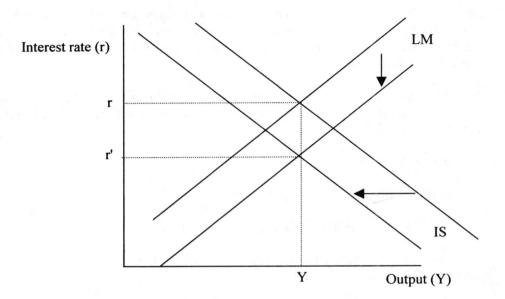

CHAPTER 10

Multiple Choice

Open economy can be confusing sometimes. Here are some definitions.

The current account:

> Includes:
> Net exports = exports – imports.
> Official transfers
> Net investment income
> Increases with greater domestic income.

The private capital account:

> inflows – outflows of financial capital.
> Decreases with higher interest rates.

Private balance of payments is the sum of the current account and the private capital account.

A surplus implies the quantity of currency demand exceeds quantity supplied.

1. c. A balance of payments imbalance implies that the quantity of currency demanded does not equal quantity supplied. If the exchange rate is flexible, it will adjust to restore balance.

2. b. In order to maintain a fixed exchange rate, the government must intervene in the market for currency.

3. d. The balance of payments curve is shown below and will shift when exchange rates change.

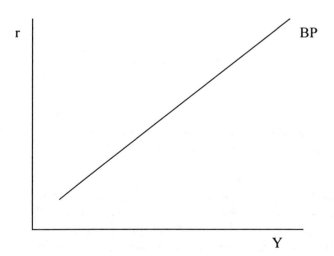

4. c. Domestic income tends to increase imports and hence decreases the current account balance. The increase in interest rates will cause outflows to decline and inflows to increase. The private capital account (inflows – outflows) will thus decrease.

5. c. A change in the interest rate will cause a movement along the curve, not a shift in the curve.

6. c. Internal balance is achieved when the IS and LM curves intersect at the desired level of output and interest rates.

7. a. External balance is achieved when the government achieves the desired exchange rate and the desired level of trade balance (if exchange rates are flexible), or desired level of balance of payments (if exchange rates are fixed).

8. b. The Mundell-Fleming model assumes perfect capital mobility and that the economy is small enough so that they have to take world interest rates as given.

9-10: In the Mundell-Fleming model, since the interest rate is set at the world interest rate and capital is perfectly mobile. The BP curve is horizontal at the real interest rate.

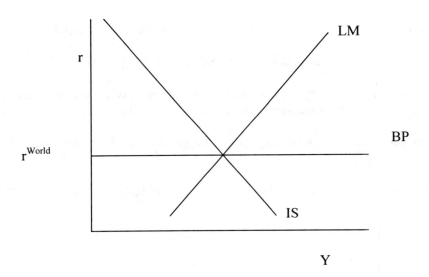

9. b. When exchange rates are fixed, expansionary fiscal policy puts upward pressure on the exchange rate and expansionary monetary policy is necessary to keep exchange rates fixed: fiscal policy is very effective.

   When exchange rates are flexible, expansionary fiscal policy will lead to an appreciation of the exchange rate and a decline in exports: fiscal policy is ineffective in this case.

10. c. When exchange rates are fixed, monetary policy changes will be immediately reversed in order to keep the exchange rates from fluctuating: monetary policy is ineffective.

When exchange rates are flexible, expansionary monetary policy causes currency depreciation and hence a shift in the IS curve in addition to the shift in the LM curve: monetary policy is very effective.

True/False/Uncertain

1. False. A balance of payments deficit implies that the quantity of currency supplied exceeds the quantity demanded and hence there will be a decline in the value of the currency: a currency depreciation. This will lead to a decline in imports as foreign goods become more expensive to domestic consumers.

2. Uncertain. This statement is almost true. For a country to run a *current account surplus*, the capital account must be in deficit. The current account equals the trade deficit plus official transfers and net investment income. If official transfers and net investment were both zero, the statement would be true.

3. Uncertain. This statement is true if the economy is small—that is, it is not large enough to affect international credit markets. If there is any risk involved, there may be an additional risk premium which increases the domestic interest rate – by following policies that change the risk premium, the interest rate may be indirectly affected.

4. Uncertain. If there is a fixed exchange rate, the statement is true. If the exchange rate is flexible, the Fed can use monetary policy to affect the exchange rate and hence net exports and output. See (9) and (10) above.

5. True. The technical requirements for an optimal currency area include: similar industries, significant labor mobility, broad range of industries, and diverse demand shocks.

Problems

1. Deriving the BP curve.

    a. As domestic income rises, people consume more goods from abroad. Exports will depend upon foreign incomes, but not domestic income.

    b. If $Y = 1,000$, the trade balance is equal to

    $$(X - M) = 100 - (50 + 0.1 \times 1,000)$$
    $$= -50.$$

    So, there is a trade deficit of 50.

If Y = 2,000, the trade balance is equal to

$$(X - M) = 100 - (50 + 0.1 \times 2,000)$$
$$= -150.$$

So, there is a trade deficit of 150.

c. The current account will balance when $X = M$, or

$$100 = 50 + 0.1\ Y,$$
$$Y = 500.$$

d. See graph below.

Current Account

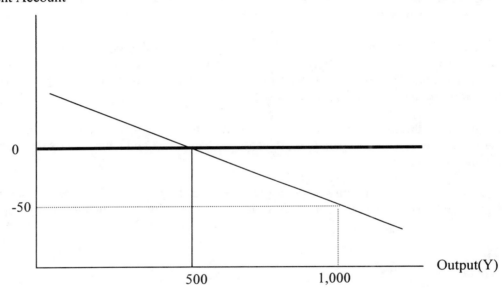

e. When the interest rate is high relative to interest rates abroad, people will tend to purchase domestic assets because they pay a higher return. This causes fewer outflows and more inflows.

f. The private capital account balance is

$$inflows - outflows = (50 + 1,000\ r) - (150 - 1,000\ r)$$
$$= 2,000\ r - 100.$$

If $r = 0.05$, the private capital account balance is 2,000 (0.05) – 100 = 0.
If $r = 0.1$, the private capital account balance is: 2,000 (0.15) – 100 = 200.

g. As found in part f, the private capital account will be in balance when r = 5%.

h. See diagram below.

Private Capital Account
Balance

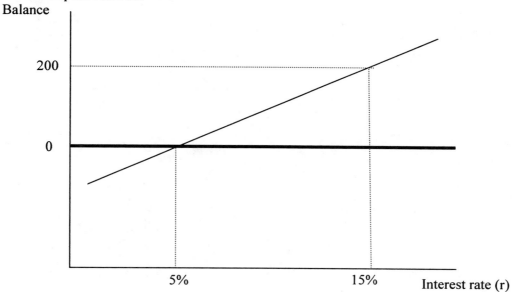

i.   If Y = 1,000, the current account balance will be –50, see part (b). Therefore, the capital account must be +50.

j.   Since the capital account is +50, the interest rate in equilibrium must be given by

$$50 = inflows - outflows$$
$$= 2,000\ r - 100.$$
$$r = 150 / 2,000$$
$$= 0.075$$

So an interest rate of 7.5% will be required to achieve balance.

k. If Y = 500 the current account balance and the capital account balance will both be 0, and the interest rate to achieve equilibrium must be: $r = 100/2,000 = 0.05 = 5\%$

1. See graph below.

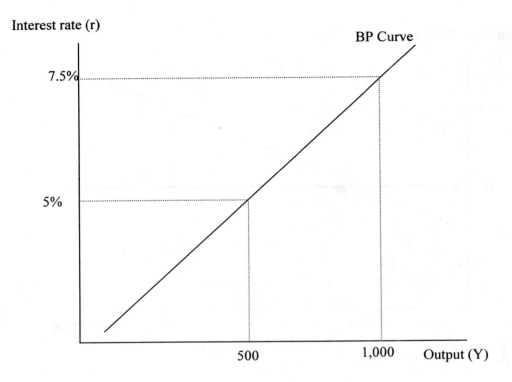

2. Open economy multiplier.

a. The equilibrium level of output is found by setting $Y = AE$.

$$
\begin{aligned}
Y &= C + I_0 + G_0 + (X_0 - M) \\
Y &= C_0 + mpc\,(Y\text{-}T_0) + I_0 + G_0 + [X_0 - (M_0 + m\,Y)] \\
Y - mpcY + mY &= C_0 - mpc\,(T_0) + I_0 + G_0 + (X_0 - M_0) \\
Y &= [1/(1\text{-}mpc+m)]\,[C_0 - mpc\,(T_0) + I_0 + G_0 + (X_0 - M_0)].
\end{aligned}
$$

Plugging in numbers, this gives:

$$
\begin{aligned}
Y &= [1/(1\text{-}0.9+0.2)]\,[100 - 0.9\,(100) + 300 + 100 + (100 - 0)] \\
Y &= 3.33\ \,[\,510\,] \\
Y &= 1,700
\end{aligned}
$$

b. Equilibrium output when $G = 200$ is

$$
\begin{aligned}
Y &= [1/(1\text{-}0.9+0.2)]\,[100 - 0.9\,(100) + 300 + 200 + (100 - 0)], \\
Y &= 2,033.
\end{aligned}
$$

Equilibrium output has thus increased by $2,033 - 1,700 = 333$.

This can also be founds as follows. $\Delta Y = 3.33\ \Delta G = 3.33\,[100] = 333$.

c.   The multiplier is $\Delta Y/\Delta G = 333/100 = 3.33$.

d.   Maybe. With no trade, the multiplier would have been 10. Because the import market absorbs some of the output from economic booms (and softens the blows from economic slowdowns), the economy will respond less to changes in autonomous expenditures.

However, when there is trade, there may be an additional source of economic shocks – namely exports. Changes in exports will be another source of possible economic shocks that might destabilize the macroeconomy.

3.   Policy in the open economy.

a.   See the diagram below. An increase in government spending will shift the IS curve to the right (1) causing an increase in output and an increase in interest rates. At the new equilibrium, however, the balance of payments is not in equilibrium – rather it is in deficit since imports have increased due to higher income. As a result, and since exchange rates are flexible, there will be a depreciation (2) and the BP curve will shift to the right.

Note that outflows have decreased and inflows have increased due to the higher interest rate, which would tend to increase the balance of payments; however, as the BP curve is drawn below, this change is not enough to offset the decline due to the change in imports. If the BP curve were drawn to be flatter than the LM curve, the effect of the interest rate would be greater than the effect of the higher output and there would be a balance of payments surplus and an appreciation in the currency.

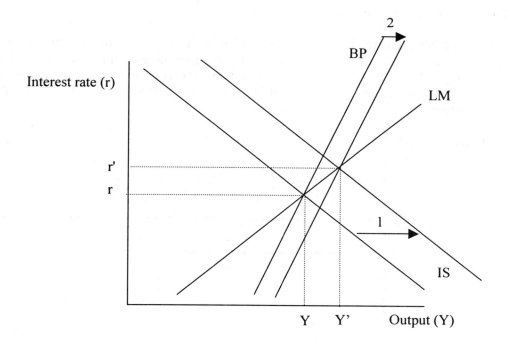

b. See diagram below. The shift in the LM curve will (1) lead to higher output and lower interest rates. At the new equilibrium, however the balance of payments is not in equilibrium – rather it is in deficit since outflows have increased and inflows have decreased due to the lower interest rate; and imports have increased due to a higher level of income. As a result, and since exchange rates are flexible, there will be a depreciation (2) and the BP curve will shift to the right.

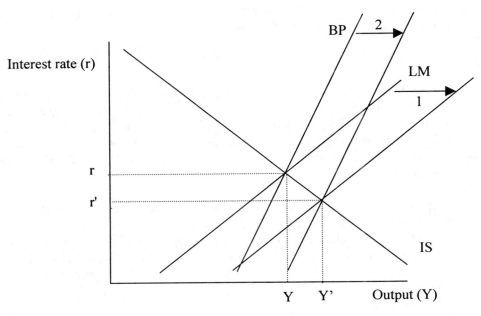

4. World interest rates in a small open economy.

a. Floating exchange rates. See diagram below. The increase in the world interest rate (1) will cause there to be downward pressure on the exchange rate since the domestic interest rate is lower than the world interest rate. The resulting depreciation will lead to an increase in net exports and a shift in the IS curve to the right (2). The net result is higher output.

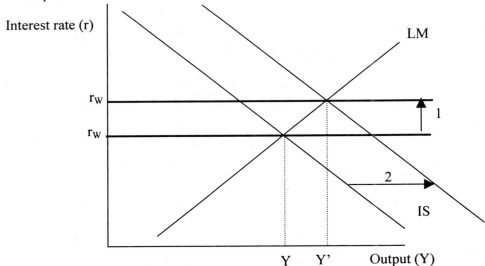

b. Fixed exchange rates. See diagram below. The increase in the world interest rate (1) will cause there to be downward pressure on the exchange rate since the domestic interest rate is lower than the world interest rate. However, in order to keep he exchange rate fixed, contractionary policy must be followed and the LM curve must shift up (2). The result is lower output.

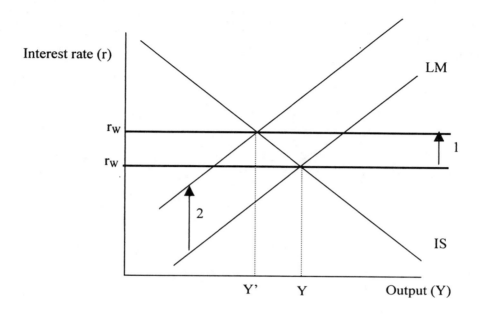

c. When exchange rates are floating (a), the government should reduce the money supply to shift the LM curve up. A shift in fiscal policy will have no effect since the IS curve will simply return to its previous position as the exchange rate changes.

When exchange rates are fixed (b), the government should follow an expansionary fiscal policy to increase output. A shift in monetary policy will not work because any change will have to be immediately reversed to keep exchange rates fixed.

Chapter 11

Multiple Choice

1. e. The AD is derived from the IS/LM model. Prices affect output through either the interest rate effect or through the international effect. Both effects cause the AD curve to slope downward.

2. c. Expansionary fiscal policy will shift the IS curve to the right, and thus cause output to be higher at any given price level. This is represented by a shift to the right of the AD curve. See graph below.

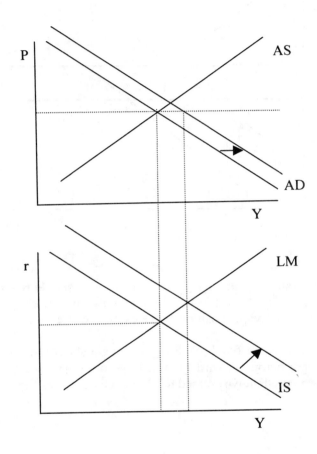

3.   c. Expansionary fiscal policy will shift the IS curve to the right, and thus cause output to be higher at any given price level. This is represented by a shift to the right of the AD curve. See graph below.

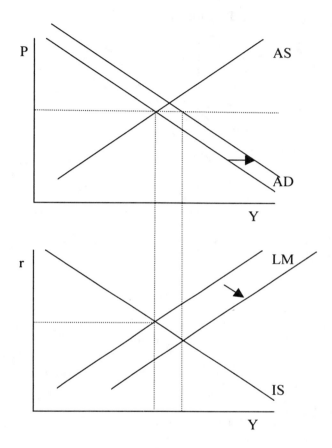

4.   e. The AD curve is derived from the IS/LM model which includes the multiplier model:

$$Y = C + I + G + (X - M),$$

Changes in any of these components (except for changes caused by price changes) will then change the AD curve. (A money supply change will impact investment through interest rates.)

5.   d. Government spending affects the AD curve, not the AS curve. Factors that shift the AS curve include: inflationary expectations, productivity, and input prices.

6.   b. In the long-run output is determined by the potential output. According to the conventional view expansionary policy will only lead to higher prices. The unconventional view mentioned in the text suggests that an AD shift might also change potential output. In this case, (c) would be the correct choice.

7.   a. When output differs from potential, expected prices differ from actual prices and inflationary expectations are changed. The adjustment to the long-run occurs when price expectations change and the AS curve shifts. See diagram below for an example of when the AD curve has shifted out.

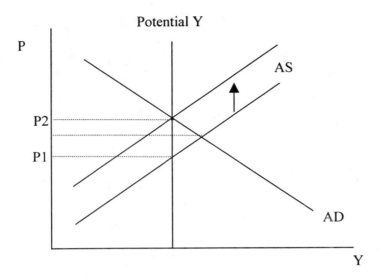

Expected prices adjust from P1 to P2.

8.   d. Sticky wages, worker misperceptions about inflation, or imperfect price information are all reasons why output might deviate from potential output.

9.   b. New growth theory focuses on technology and the supply side of the economy to try and explain why output fluctuates over time.

10. d. Rational expectations imply that people will anticipate the impact on prices of any aggregate demand policy. This will cause a shift in expected inflation and hence a shift of the AS curve that will offset the AD policy, even in the short-run. (Note: strictly speaking, this is not true. If there are nominal wage rigidities, or other kind of sticky prices then rational expectations are not sufficient to imply no effect on policy in the short-run.)

True/False/Uncertain

1.   True. See questions (2) and (3) in the multiple-choice section above. Monetary policy will shift the LM curve and hence the AD curve. Fiscal policy will shift the IS curve and also the AD curve.

2.   True. Higher prices will cause an increase in the money demand (or a decrease in the real money supply), leading to higher interest rates and lower investment. This is the interest rate mechanism for explaining why the AD curve has a negative slope.

3. False. The slope of the AS curve comes from the labor market and the use of cost-plus-markup rules. The chain of causality runs as follows:

    > Demand for goods and services increases → firms increase their demand for inputs (including labor) → since all firms have greater demand, the market price rises → the firms cost rise → prices increase since there is a markup over costs.

4. False. In the long-run the AS curve is vertical at potential output.

5. False. An increase in inflationary expectations will lead to an upward shift in the AS curve, and a recession (if we assume we started from a long-run equilibrium.) See diagram below. If price expectations shift from P1 to P3, output will fall from potential to Y2

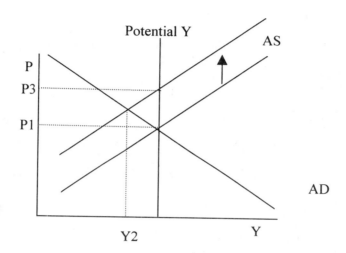

6. Uncertain. An adverse supply shock is shown above. As you can see prices are higher and output is lower. If we wish to fight the recession and increase output (at the expense of even higher prices), we can follow either policy suggested in the question—by decreasing taxes or by increasing the money supply—to shift the AD curve to the right.

    The money supply approach will lead to higher investment through lower interest rates. The tax approach will lead to greater consumption by increasing disposable income (and also a greater budget deficit). Each policy thus has a different "mix" of aggregate demand components. There is no definitive answer as to which policy is best; although the majority of economists might prefer the monetary policy approach in order to boost investment.

Problems

1. Using the AD/AD model. Directions of changes are shown here. Graphs of each case are below.
   Key: (++) large increase; (+) increase; (0) no change; (-) decrease; (--) large decrease.
   The changes are indicated from the initial long-run equilibrium.

   a. Tax cut. Shifts the IS to the right. Shifts AD to the right.

	Short-run	Long-run
Output	(+)	(0)
Prices	(+)	(++)
Consumption	(+)	(+)
Interest rates	(+)	(+)
Investment	(-)	(-)

   b. Decrease in government expenditures. Shifts the IS to the left. Shifts AD to the left.

	Short-run	Long-run
Output	(-)	(0)
Prices	(-)	(--)
Consumption	(-)	(0)
Interest rates	(-)	(-)
Investment	(+)	(+)

   c. Money supply increase. Shifts the LM to the right. Shifts AD to the right.

	Short-run	Long-run
Output	(+)	(0)
Prices	(+)	(++)
Consumption	(+)	(0)
Interest rates	(-)	(0)
Investment	(+)	(0)

   d. Money supply increase, government expenditure decline. Shifts the LM to the right, and the IS to the left. AD shift will depend upon the relative magnitudes of the IS and LM shifts.

	Short-run	Long-run
Output	(+) or (-)	(0)
Prices	(+) or (-)	(++) or (--)
Consumption	(+) or (-)	(0)
Interest rates	(-)	(-)
Investment	(+)	(+)

   e. Tax cut, increased spending, and decline in money supply. Shifts the LM to the left, and the IS to the right. AD shift will depend upon the relative magnitudes of the IS and LM shifts.

	Short-run	Long-run
Output	(+) or (-)	(0)
Prices	(+) or (-)	(++) or (--)
Consumption	(+) or (-)	(+)
Interest rates	(+)	(+)
Investment	(-)	(-)

Graphs: The solutions for parts (a) and (b) will carefully detail the short-run relation between the IS/LM model and the AS/AD model. The solutions for (c)-(e) will show the models separately and will be not as detailed about the interrelations between the two models.

d. 1) The IS curve shifts by the multiplier times mpc ΔT. 2) This shifts the AD curve to the right by the amount given by the interscection of the IS/LM graph. 3) The increase in price causes a shift up in the LM curve, and equilibrium output is reached.

In the long-run, the AS curve will rise, and the LM curve will continue to shift up until output returns to potential.

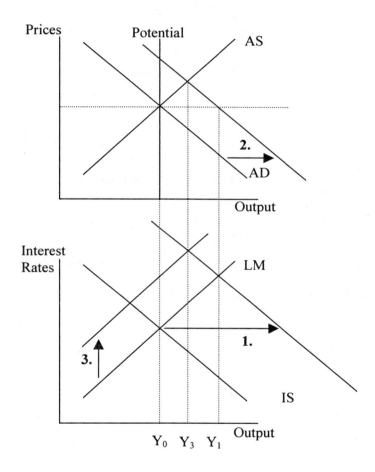

e. The decrease in government spending will do the exact reverse of the decrease in taxes (except in the case of consumption). 1) The IS curve shifts by the multiplier times ΔG. 2) This shifts the AD curve to the left by the amount given by the interscection of the IS/LM graph. 3) The decrease in price causes a shift down in the LM curve, and equilibrium output is reached.

In the long-run, the AS curve will shift down, and the LM curve will contiune to shift down untill output returns to potential.

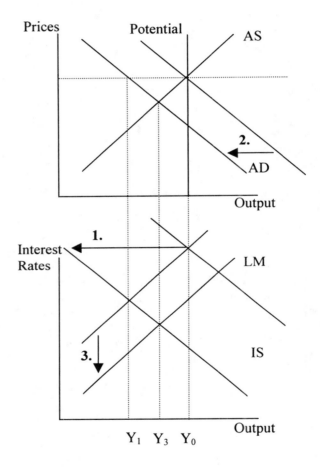

f. See diagrams below. In the short-run there is an increase in output (1), but in the long-run, the LM shifts back (2).

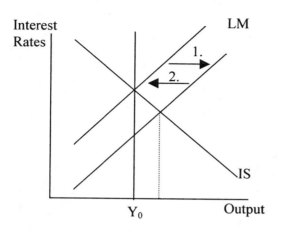
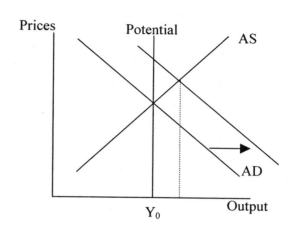

g. See diagrams below. In the short-run there will be a shift in both the IS and LM curves. The AD curve could shift in either direction (or neither) depending upon the strength of the policy moves and the shapes of the curves. The graph here shows a net increase in AD. In the long-run, the AS and LM curves will shift to return output to potential.

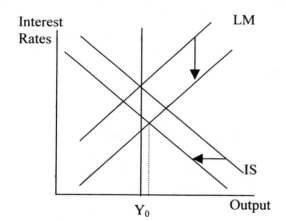
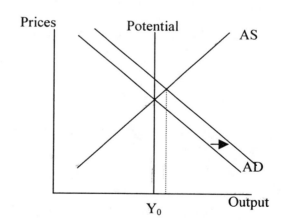

h. See diagrams below. In the short-run there will be a shift in both the IS and LM curves. The AD curve could again shift in either direction (or neither) depending upon the strength of the policy moves and the shapes of the curves. The graph here shows a net decrease in AD. In the long-run, the AS and LM curves will shift to return output to potential.

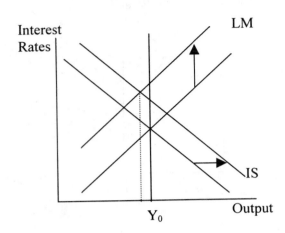

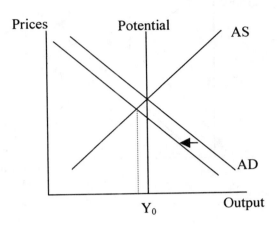

2. Crowding out in the long-run. As usual, equilibrium is given by setting Y = AE and solving for Y. In this case this yield the following equation for equilibrium output.

$$Y = 1/(1\text{-}mpc) \; [C_0 - mpc(T_0) + (I_0 - 1000 \; r) + G_0 + (X_0 - M_0).$$

a. Plugging in numbers we get that

$$Y = 10 \; [\; 100 - 0.9(100) + (300 - 100) + 100 + 0]$$
$$= 10 \; [\; 310 \;]$$
$$= 3,100$$

b. If government spending increases, and there is no change in interest rates, output will drop by

$$\Delta Y = 1/(1\text{-}mpc) \; [\Delta G] = 10 \; [100] = 1,000.$$

So output will increase by 1,000 to 4,100.

c.   On the IS/LM diagram, this means that the IS curve will shift to the right by 1,000. See below

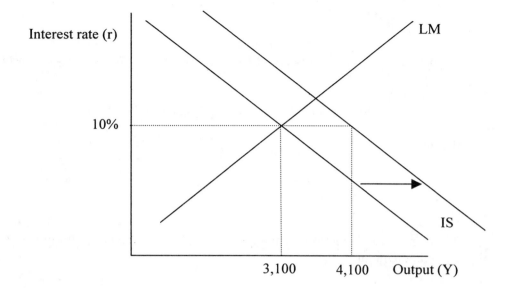

d. The new equilibrium output if interest rates increased to 15% will be found as follows:

$$Y = 10 [100 - 0.9(100) + (300 - 150) + 200 + 0]$$
$$= 10 [360]$$
$$= 3,600$$

Alternatively, we could note that an increase in interest rates will cause a reduction on investment of

$$\Delta I = \Delta(300 - 1,000r) = -1,000 \, \Delta r = -1,000 \, (0.05) = -50.$$

And then,

$$\Delta G = 1/(1\text{-}mpc) \, \Delta I,$$
$$= 10 [-50]$$
$$= -500.$$

This then is the reduction from 4,100 to 3,600. This new equilibrium is show in the following diagram

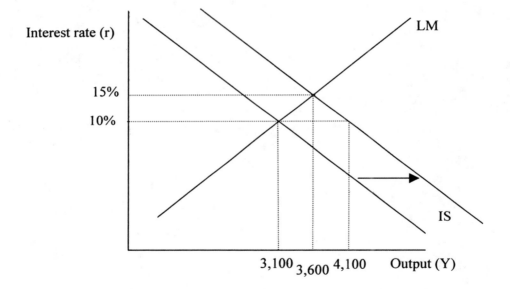

e. The net effect of the government spending increase was an increase in output of 500, and a decrease in investment of 50.

f. The AD curve will shift to the right as shown below. In the short-run (1) output and prices will increase. In the long-run, the AS curve will shift up and output will return to potential (2).

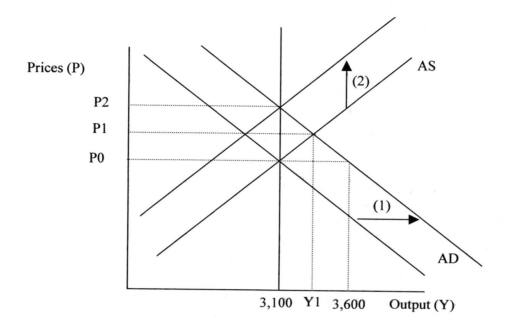

g. The when prices rise, so too will the demand for nominal money balances. This is represented by an increase in the money demand curve. The result is a higher interest rate. See graph below.

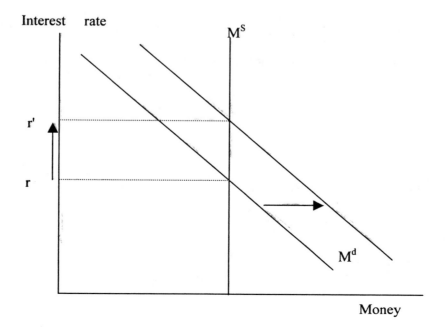

h.   The LM curve shifts upwards because of the increased money demand, leading to lower output and even higher interest rates.

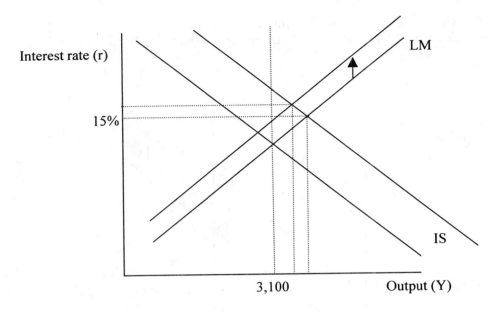

i.   In the long-run, prices will increase further and output will return to the level of potential output: 3,100.

j.   Since we know output must be 3,100, we can use this to find investment:

Y $= 1/(1\text{-}mpc)\ [C_0 - mpc(T_0) + (I_0 - 1000\ r) + G_0 + (X_0 - M_0)$.
$3,100$ $= 10$ $[\ 100 - 0.9(100) + I + 200 + 0]$
$3,100$ $= 10\ [210 + I]$

Which solves to $I = 100$. Since $I = 300 - 1000r$, this gives $r = 20\%$

k.   Note that investment was initially equal to 200. So the initial increase of 100 in government spending lead to a 100 reduction in investment!

3. Active Fed.
   a. A tax cut would shift the AD curve out (1). Since this would tend to raise prices, the Fed will raise interest rates and shift the AD curve back to its original position. See graph.

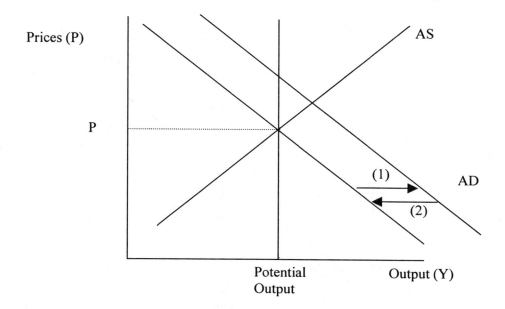

b.   An adverse AS shock (1) is shown in the graph below. To prevent prices from rising the Fed will increase interest rates and shift the AD curve to the left (2).

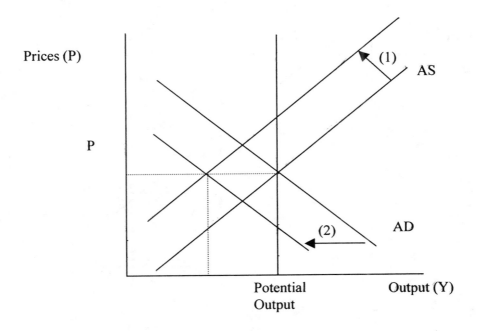

c.   In the case of the demand shock, the Fed's policy will prevent inflation. In the case of the supply shock, the Fed can prevent inflation, but only at the expense of having output drop by a large amount. Whether or not this is a good idea depends upon the relative cost of inflation versus low output.

d.   This policy might work well if the economy is subject primarily to demand shocks and not supply shocks.

4. Expectations.
    a. See diagram.
    b. See diagram, AD shifts out (1).
    c. In the new equilibrium, actual prices P_1 are greater that expected prices P^e_1.
    d. See diagram, the AS curve shifts up (2) to reflect the higher price expectations.
    e. Actual prices P_2 are greater that expected prices P^e_2. The AS curve again shifts up (3).
    f. In each year, the expected prices are below the actual price.
    g. The do not seem to be reasonable since people are making the same mistake year after year.
    h. If people were more sophisticated, they would have price expectations that were greater than the simple rule presented here. The adjustment towards the long-run equilibrium would be faster if this were the case. In the extreme, the adjustment would be instantaneous and there would be no increase in output even in the short-run.

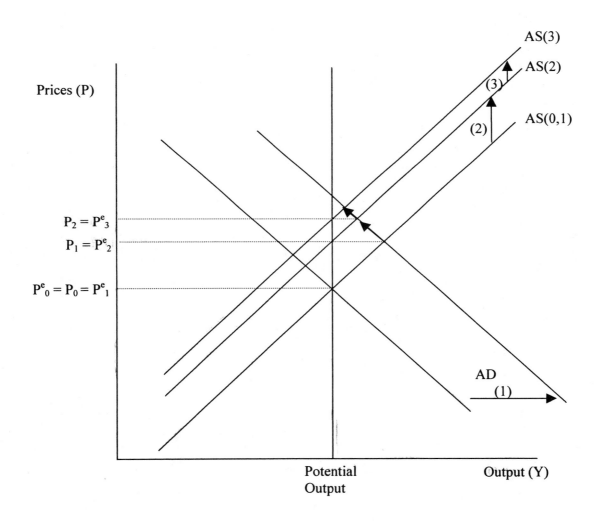

5.   Which shock?

   a.   Shift out in the AD curve. In the short-run there will be an increase in prices and an increase in output. In the long-run output will return to potential and prices will rise further.

   b.   If the monetary policy shock was strong enough, it will have the same effect as in part (a)

   c.   The AS curve would shift to the right, (1), leading to higher output and lower prices in the short-run. In the long-run output and prices would return to their precious level, (2). See diagram below.

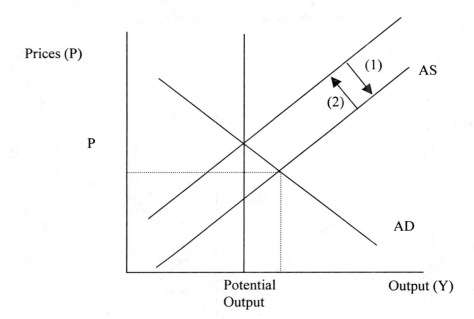

d. A permanent increase in the level of potential output would shift the AS curve as well as the potential output line (see graph). This would lead to higher output and lower prices in the short-run. In addition, in the long-run prices would fall ever farther, and output would increase even more than in the short-run. See diagram.

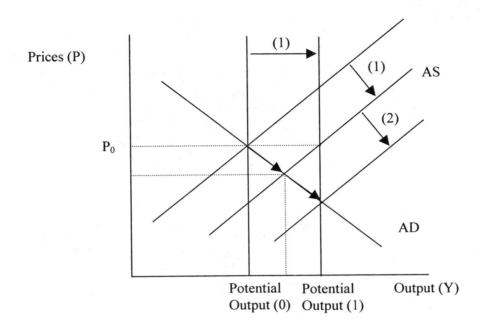

If inflation was not increasing, then we can rule out the demand shocks. After several years we can look to see what happened to prices and output. If output continued to increase and inflation continued to fall, that would imply an increase in potential output, (d). If prices began to rise again and output returned to its previous level, we could conclude that it was a onetime shift in aggregate supply. (Of course, this assumes no additional shocks hit the economy in the meantime!)

If there were no change in inflation, then an increase in the permanent level of output would be consistent with the permanent shift in potential output as well as one of the demand side policies.

This outcome is shown in the following diagram.

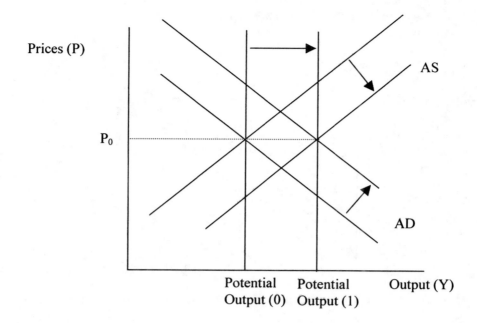

Chapter 12

Multiple Choice

1. b. Intertemporal choice is about decisions made over time, whether they are about consumption, investment, or whether to study on a Friday night.

2. b. The present value is $PV = \$110 / (1 + 0.1) = \$110 / 1.1 = \$100$.

3. b. The average propensity to consume, $apc = C / Y$. Empirically it looks as though the average propensity to consume is constant if measured over the long-run. In the short-run, the apc varies with income.

    Long-run apc = C^{LR} / Y^d = 0.9,
    Short-run apc = C^{SR} / Y^d = 26.5 / Y^d + 0.75.

4. e. The permanent income hypothesis assumes that people look at their earning over their lifetime and that they like to smooth their income. All the other results follow from these assumptions.

5. a. Like the permanent income hypothesis, the life-cycle hypothesis makes the same assumption that people like to smooth their consumption over time. (Actually, the smoothing assumption can be derived by looking at individuals' intertemporal consumption decisions and making certain assumptions about the utility function.)

6. d. The life cycle and permanent income theories do not perfectly fit the facts. However, the idea that people look into the future to make decisions about consumption in the present is important when analyzing policy.

7. b. The mei is defined by the following equation where C is the cost of the project, and Xt is the marginal profit generated by the project in year t:

    $C = X1 / (1+mei) + X2 / (1+mei)^2 + X3 / (1+mei)^3 + ...$

8. c. If the mei is greater than the interest rate, the present value of the project's profits will exceed the cost, and the investment should be made.

9. b. The expected value is $100*0.2 + 1,000*0.8 = 20 + 800 = 820$.

10. d. The wealth effect describes another way that the Fed can influence the economy. A monetary policy that lowers interest rates will increase the present value of stock dividends, and thus push up stock prices. The higher prices means that stockowners now have greater wealth. To the extent that they increase consumption as a result, there will be a shift to the right of the IS curve. This makes monetary policy even more powerful.

True/False/Uncertain

1. False. The price and the interest rate of a bond are inversely related. For a out year bond

    $$P_B = X/(1+r),$$

    where X is the face value of the bond.

2. False. A firm should invest if Tobin's-q is greater than 1.

    $$Tobin's\ q = \frac{market\ value\ of\ current\ capital}{cost\ of\ replacement\ capital.}$$

    If q is greater than 1 the stock market valuation of the firm's existing capital is greater than the replacement cost – and it is therefore worthwhile for the firm to add more capital by investing.

3. False. Historically, there have been cases where shock prices have likely followed a speculative bubble pattern. A speculative bubble occurs when investors buy stocks solely on the belief that they can sell them for a higher price in the future.

    It is sometimes hard to tell the difference between a price in a speculative bubble and a price that looks at the present value of future dividends. This is because the present value theory hinges on the *expected* future dividends, which are hard, if not impossible, to measure.

4. False. The wealth effect makes monetary policy *more* effective. See the answer to problem (10) above.

5. Uncertain. Riskier bonds do tend to pay a higher interest rate to compensate the purchaser of the bond for the extra default risk. However, longer maturity bonds usually tend to pay a *higher* interest rate. Occasionally, the yield curve becomes inverted; in which case, the longer bonds will pay a lower interest rate.

Problems

1. Present value

    a. If $r = 10\%$:

        $$PV = 1,000 / (1+r) + 1,000 / (1+r)^2 + 1,000 / (1+r)^3.$$
        $$PV = 2,486.85$$

    b. If r = 5%: PV = 2723.25.

2. Given a fixed payment X, the project will be profitable if

$$\$1,000 < X/(1+r) + X/(1+r)^2 + \dots$$
$$\$1,000 < X/r,$$
$$X > \$1,000\,r.$$

a. If r = 10%, the project will be profitable if the payment is greater than $1,000r = $100.
b. If r = 10%, the project will be profitable if the payment is greater than $1,000r = $50.

3. Finding the mei.

a. The mei is given by 100 = 110 / (1+mei), so mei = (110 / 100) – 1 = 0.1 or 10%
b. The mei is 100 = 100 / (1+mei) + 100 / (1+mei)^2, which gives an mei of 0.13 or 13%.
c. The mei is 100 = 10 / (1+mei) + 10 / (1+mei)^2 + … = 10 / mei, or mei = 0.1 or 10%.

4. Stock prices.

$$PV_1 = X_1/(1+r) + X_2/(1+r)^2 + X_3/(1+r)^3 + \dots .$$

a. Next year the present value will be

$$PV_2 = X_2/(1+r) + X_3/(1+r)^2 + X_4/(1+r)^3 + \dots .$$

b. Using the hint and multiplying PV2 by (1+r) gives:

$(1+r)\,PV_2$ $= (1+r)\,[\,X_2/(1+r) + X_3/(1+r)^2 + X_4/(1+r)^3 + \dots\,]$
$(1+r)\,PV$ $= X_2/(1+r)^2 + X_3/(1+r)^3 + + X_4/(1+r)^4 \dots .$
$(1+r)\,PV_2$ $= PV_1 - X_1/(1+r)$
PV_2 $= (1+r)\,PV_1 - X_1$

c. The percentage change is then found by using the above equation:

$$\frac{PV_2 - PV_1}{PV_1} = \frac{(1+r)\,PV_1 - X_1 - PV_1}{PV_1}$$

$$(PV_2 - PV_1)/PV_1 = r + X_1/PV_1$$

$$\%\Delta PV_1 = r + X_1/PV_1$$

d. This equation makes sense because the return you get from a stock (if there is no risk) ought to equal the return to bonds, which is the interest rate. The equation above can be written as

$$r = \%\Delta PV_1 - X_1/PV_1$$

Which says that the interest rate equals the rate of price increase (the capital gain) plus the dividend rate. In other words, the money you could make from buying a bond is equal to the money you can make from buying a stock, which is equal to the percentage price increase plus the money you make from dividends.

5. Life cycle consumption.

    a.   An increase in income of $50 in year will lead to a total lifetime increase of 20 times $50 or $1,000. Since you will live for 50 more years, you will increase consumption by $1,000/50 = $20. This means that during your working years you will save an additional $30, and during retirement you will dissave by $20 more.

    b.   A one-time increase will lead to a $1,000/50 = $20 increase in yearly consumption. This means that when you receive the bonus, your savings will increase by $980, and every year thereafter, you will save $20 less.

    c.   The income earned from the 1,000 would allow you (in part b) to consume more that the extra $20 per year. This will also be true in case (a), but not to the same degree since savings have not increased as much as in (b). In addition, if the interest rate were positive, the present value of the 50 stream of income in part (a) would be less that the instant 1,000 as in part (b).

6. Good News?

    a.   If GDP is high, we might expect that companies are producing and selling a high amount and earning higher total profits in the future.

    b.   If the Fed wishes to keep prices stable, they might wish to tighten monetary policy by raising the interest rate.

    c.   The present value equation for stock is:

$$PV_1 = X_1 / (1+r) + X_2 / (1+r)^2 + X_3 / (1+r)^3 + \ldots .$$

       If profits are high, then we can expect higher dividends X_t in the future, so this might suggest that prices will rise. However, if we expect interest rate to go up, this would suggest that prices would fall. So prices could go either direction depending upon the strength of each effect.

    d.   If the stock market were below potential, we might expect that the Fed would be less likely to react to the GDP news with an interest rate increase. So, the news announcement would likely increase stock prices.

Chapter 13

Multiple Choice

1. c. The Secretary of the Treasury does not participate directly in the formulation of monetary policy. The Treasury, however, is in charge of exchange rate policy, so some policy must be coordinated between the two agencies.

2. a. You should know this by now!

3. b. The money multiplier arises because some of the money given to banks in the form of deposits is then lent out to borrowers; thus, banks create money. The size of the simple money multiplier (if no currency or extra reserves are held) is *1/r* where *r* is the reserve ratio.

4. c. Zero inflation is an *ultimate* target, not an intermediate target.

5. d. The time consistency problem arises when policy must be made year after year. If people base current decisions on their beliefs of the future, then their belief of what policymakers will do in the future will impact the economy today.

    The time consistency problem is when policymakers have an incentive to announce one thing and then renege on that policy in the future.

True/False/Uncertain

1. False. The Federal open market committee (FOMC) makes monetary policy decisions – the chairman counts only as one vote. In practice, however, the chairman of the Fed has usually played an important leadership role in steering the direction of policy.

2. False. The Fed increases the money supply by *buying* bonds.

    When a Fed purchases bonds, money moves from the Fed's vault (or bank account) to the hands of private individuals; increasing the money supply.

3. True. The complex money multiplier is given by:

    Complex money multiplier = (1 + c) / (r + c + e),

    where *c* is the cash-deposit ratio, *r* is the reserve requirement, and *e* is the excess reserve-deposit ratio.

    So, as *e* increases, the money supply decreases.

    Intuitively, this can be understood as follows: the greater the amount of excess reserves that banks hold, the less money they lend out, and the less money they create.

4. False. The Fed often has to act defensively, that is, they engage in open market transactions not to change the interest rate, but rather to keep it from changing.

5.   False. The Taylor rule looks at real output in addition to inflation. The Taylor rule suggest that:

Federal funds rate = 2   + current inflation
                                    + 0.5 (actual inflation – desired inflation)
                                    + 0.5 (percent deviation of aggregate output from potential).

Problems

1.   Money multiplier.

   a.   The money multiplier, in this case, is given by 1/r. So a 10% required reserve ratio would correspond to a money multiplier of 1/0.1 = 10. If r = 0.02, the money multiplier would be 1/0.2 = 5.
   b.   The money supply = money multiplier x monetary base. So the money supply will go from $10 trillion to $5 trillion.
   c.   If the money multiplier was 5 and the Fed wanted to maintain a money supply of $10 trillion, they would have to increase the money base from $1 trillion to $2 trillion.

2.   Supply and demand for money.

   a.   If the demand for money grows at 1%, the money supply must grow at the same rate to prevent interest rates from rising. Since

   money supply = money multiplier x *monetary base*

   we know that,

   %Δ money supply = %Δ money multiplier + %Δmonetary base

   So, if we want the money supply to grow at 1%, then the monetary base must grow at 1 percent as well.

3.   To answer this question, it will be helpful to know the complex money multiplier, which is equal to

   Money multiplier = (1 + c) / (r + e + c).

   a.   If there is an increase in *c*, the money multiplier will decrease. (To find this you can simply plug in numbers for each of the numbers (note that r + e must be less than 1), or do some simple calculus to find:

   (δmm / δc) = (e + c – 1) / (e + c + r)^2 < 0 since e + c < 1.

   Because of the drop in the money multiplier, the money supply will decrease if the fed does nothing.

   b.   If the banks think people will want to take money out of the bank, they may wish to hold a greater percentage of their assets in reserve. So there may be an increase in *e*. This will lead again to a smaller money multiplier and a decrease in the money supply.

c. If the Fed wished to keep interest rates unchanged, they would have had to increase the money base to compensate for the factors above.

4. Taylor rule.

The Taylor rule is given by

Federal funds rate = 2 + current inflation
+ 0.5 (actual inflation – desired inflation)
+ 0.5 (percent deviation of aggregate output from potential)

a. Using the Taylor rule, the target rate is:

Federal funds target $= 2 + 4 + 0.5\ (4 - 2) = 7\%$

b. Using the Taylor rule with the new potential rate we get

Federal funds target $= 2 + 4 + 0.5\ (4 - 2) + 0.5\ (4) = 9\%$

In this case we would expect the federal funds rate to increase in the near future.

Chapter 14

Multiple Choice

1. b. The cash flow method of accounting counts revenue and expenditures when they are spent. An alternative would be to separate the budget into a capital expenditure budget and a current expenditure budget. Entries into the capital budget reflect investment expenditures, which are intended to generate returns in the future.

2. a. The largest off-budget item is Social Security, which is currently running a large surplus. The on-budget surplus (or deficit) may be better measure of current policy decisions since off-budget items are usually the result of past policy decisions. Social Security was designated as off-budget in part because the program represents promises to pay benefits in the future.

3. d. The government budget constraint is given by:

$$\text{Total spending} <= \text{taxes} + \text{newly issued bonds} + \text{newly printed money,}$$
$$G <= T + \Delta B + \Delta M.$$

Interest payments are included in total spending.

4. b. About one third of spending is discretionary, and two thirds is mandatory. Mandatory spending are expenditures authorized by permanent laws and primarily consist of Social Security, Medicare, and interest payments. In practice, much of discretionary spending does not vary much from year to year. The largest component of discretionary spending is national defense.

5. c. As the population ages, there are fewer working people per retired person. Since Social Security is (mostly) a pay-as-you-go program—current workers pay for the benefits given to current retires—an aging population creates a financial problem. A real problem is that in the future, there will a smaller percentage of the population producing goods and services.

True/False/Uncertain

1. Uncertain. Budget deficits through the crowding out effect tend to raise interest rates and lower investment. However, there may also be political problems with allowing the government to maintain a significant amount of assets in the private market. In addition, the Federal government may wish to borrow to invest in the future in much the same way as an individual might borrow money to go to college—borrowing money today to improve the situation in the future. This may lead us to think about a using a current spending budget versus a capital expenditure budget.

   Finally, if the government wishes to fight a recession, they may need to reduce taxes and/or increase spending to increase economic growth. In this case, a deficit would be a necessary side effect to expansionary fiscal policy.

2. False. It is possible to have a primary budget balance or surplus and have a deficit in the overall budget. This may be the case if interest payments are large. The primary budget is equal to total tax revenues minus total expenditure excluding interest payments. When interest payments are large, the primary budget balance gives a better indication of the balance between current spending and revenue since interest payments are a result of past deficits.

3. False. The real debt increases when there is a deficit, and decreases with inflation. So the real debt may decrease if inflation is high and the deficit is small. The relation between the real surplus and the nominal surplus and inflation is as follows:

    Real surplus = nominal surplus + (inflation x total debt)

4. True. About 88% of total expenditures are financed with tax revenue. The rest is financed with borrowing (11%) and seigniorage (1%).

5. Uncertain. The long lag in the process makes it hard to fine-tune the economy, but it may be useful if a more blunt tool is needed, say, in the case of severe or prolonged recession. In addition, setting up the appropriate fiscal regime (such as setting up automatic stabilizers) can have important consequences for economic performance.

Problems

1. Real budget surplus.

    Real Surplus = nominal surplus + inflation x total debt

    a. Real Surplus = - 50 billion + 0.1 (1,000 billion)
        = - 50 billion + 100 billion
        = 50 billion.

    So there is a real surplus of 50 billion.

2. Debt policy.

    a. Inflation will tend to lead the real value of the *existing* debt to decrease. However, if inflation is high, lenders will ask for a high nominal interest rate and so the nominal surplus will be lower than otherwise. Inflation by itself will not allow the government to reduce the real debt.

        However, if the inflation were unexpected, then the treasury bonds would have been sold at a low nominal rate, and the nominal surplus will not immediately be affected by inflation, allowing the real debt to decrease.

    b. If the higher inflation was indeed unexpected and the real debt was reduced via the higher inflation, there would be some winners and loser. The losers would be the creditors of the U.S. government who are receiving a lower real interest rate than what they were expecting. Recall that a large proportion of these people are foreigners. In addition creditors in general will lose from the unexpected inflation.

        The winners are the taxpayers (who hold little fixed interest bearing assets) who will have to pay off a smaller real debt. In addition borrowers will also benefit from the unexpected inflation because of the implied lower real rate on their existing fixed rate loans.

        There is one final twist. If the government does try to reduce the debt via inflation, this may raise the risk premium on the government debt, making it more costly to borrow in the future.

3. Debt to GDP ratio.

    a. If the primary budget were balanced, the deficit would be equal to interest payments which in this case are 2% of $1 trillion

$$
\begin{aligned}
\text{Real surplus} \quad &= \text{nominal surplus} + \text{inflation} \times \text{total debt} \\
&= -0.02 \; \$1 \text{ trillion} + 0 \\
&= -\$20 \text{ Billion}
\end{aligned}
$$

So the real debt would be growing by $20 Billion, or 2%.

    b. The growth rate of the debt to GDP ratio *(Debt/Y)* is

$$
\begin{aligned}
\%\Delta(\text{Debt}/Y) \quad &= \%\Delta\text{Debt} - \%\Delta Y. \\
&= 2\% - 3\% \\
&= -1\%
\end{aligned}
$$

    c. The government could run a primary deficit of 1% of the total debt, or $10 billion, without increasing the debt to GDP ratio.

We find this by noting that from (b), the debt to GDP ratio will not change if the growth rate of the debt is equal to the growth rate of GDP, or 3%.

This implies that the deficit cannot be more than 3% of the current debt. Since 2% of the debt is paid out in interest payments, this leaves 1% of the debt with which to run a primary budget deficit.

4.   Political business cycles

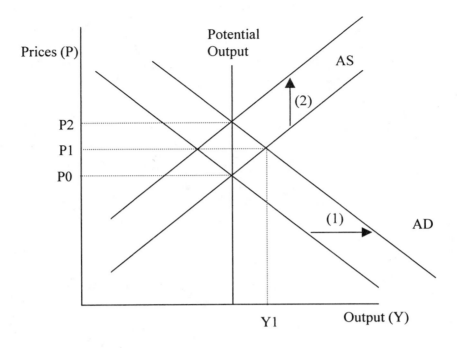

a.   See diagram above. The AD curve will shift out (1) prior to the election leading to higher output and higher prices. In the long-run, presumably after the election, prices will increase further an output will fall back to the natural rate.

b.   If the fiscal policy were expected by the public. People would anticipate the price increase and the AS curve would shift just prior to the election and at the same time as the shift in the AD curve: (1) and (2) would happen at the same time. The result would be higher prices in the short-run and the long-run, and there would be no increase in output, even in the short-run.